Out of the Dark

Out of the Dark

MY JOURNEY THROUGH THE SHADOWS TO FIND GOD'S JOY

MANDISA

with Suzanne Gosselin
Foreword by Natalie Grant

FRANKLIN, TENNESSEE

K-LOVE BOOKS

5700 West Oaks Blvd
Rocklin, CA 95765

Printed in the United States of America.

First edition: 2022
10 9 8 7 6 5 4 3 2 1

ISBN: 978-1-954201-00-2 (Hardcover)
ISBN: 978-1-954201-01-9 (E-book)
ISBN: 978-1-954201-06-4 (Audiobook)

Publisher's Cataloging-in-Publication data

Names: Mandisa, 1976-, author. | Gosselin, Suzanne Hadley, author. | Grant,
Natalie, D., foreword author.
Title: Out of the dark : my journey through the shadows to find God's joy /
Mandisa ; with Suzanne Gosselin ; foreword by Natalie Grant.
Description: Nashville, TN: K-LOVE Books, 2021.
Identifiers: ISBN: 978-1-954201-00-2 (hardcover) | 978-1-954201-01-9 (ebook) |
978-1-954201-06-4 (audio)
Subjects: LCSH Mandisa, 1976-. | Contemporary Christian musicians—United
States—Biography. | Women—Biography. | Christian life. | BISAC RELIGION
/ Christian Living / Personal Memoirs | BIOGRAPHY & AUTOBIOGRAPHY /
Music | BIOGRAPHY & AUTOBIOGRAPHY / Entertainment & Performing Arts
Classification: LCC ML420.M2185 2021 | DDC 277.3/0825/092–dc23

Cover design by two line || Studio.
Interior design and typesetting by PerfecType, Nashville, TN.

To Kisha

CONTENTS

FOREWORD

My friendship with Mandisa goes back more than a decade now. From the moment we met, we shared an instant connection over our love for the same kind of music—soulful, big-voiced singers who inspired us as vocalists. It didn't take long to realize that we had a lot more in common than just our musical tastes. We are also women with strong personalities, who have no problem speaking our minds! And through the years, we've also discovered we've faced similar battles. Our struggles may stem from different circumstances, but we have wrestled with the same things: fear, anxiety, and depression.

My sweet friend and I have both come to realize that we are not alone. So many are battling similar dark emotions that rage in their hearts and minds. Mandisa's *Out of the Dark* is an honest account that will illuminate the truth: that your mind and your heart are precious to Jesus.

It will equip you with the knowledge that God is bigger than any circumstance you face.

As you will soon experience, Mandisa's faith is infectious. And when she shares with you what is on her heart, you want to do all you can to be a part of her story. Her transparency is a constant invitation to draw near to Jesus. When she told me about her desperate desire to see her brother, John, come to know Jesus, I decided to join my faith with hers. Every day at nine a.m., an alarm would go off on my phone, and the words "Pray for John" would pop up on my screen. And that's exactly what I did each and every day. I prayed for John. You'll have to read this book to find out how God answered that prayer, but let's just say He did not disappoint.

Again and again, I've witnessed Mandisa's willingness to play a part in someone else's healing, either physical or spiritual, regardless of the cost. In fact, I have never met anyone who champions others like she does. She is a cheerleader in the most genuine ways. In her moments of great success, she often turns the attention away from her talent to shine the spotlight on those around her.

Her faithfulness in sharing her battle with depression is another example of her selfless love for others. Her openness and vulnerability in telling her story demonstrate her huge heart and confidence in the healing power of our God. *Out of the Dark* invites you into that story and shows the way to that healing. This book is not a quick fix; in fact, one of my favorite aspects of this story is that Mandisa is still on her journey. She doesn't have it all figured out. She openly invites us to peek into her life and is candid about how, as a follower of Jesus, you can believe the truth one day and wake up the next having fallen for another lie. By revealing her own struggles, she helps us see that God is the One who does the work and leads us to true and lasting freedom. We don't need a quick fix; we just need Jesus. Every moment. Every day. And in each chapter, Mandisa leads us back to this truth.

I know *Out of the Dark* will be a lifeline to those who, like us, have struggled with their mental health. She is not afraid to share the hard times she has walked through, and I am so very proud of my friend's courage and vulnerability. Wherever you find yourself on your life journey, in this book you will find wisdom and practical advice to help you find contentment with who God made you to be and the courage to take Him at His word.

I understand how lonely the dark is. My testimony, and the testimony Mandisa shares in this book, is that only the Lord can bring you out of that darkness. As Mandisa shares her low points from her journey in the dark, it becomes evident that she trusts the Lord to be her light. We want Him to be your light too. And I believe Mandisa, through her bravery and transparency, will serve as a guide, showing many the way out of the dark.

—Natalie Grant

one

OVERCOMER

You're an overcomer
Stay in the fight 'til the final round
You're not going under
'Cause God is holding you right now
You might be down for a moment
Feeling like it's hopeless
That's when He reminds you
That you're an overcomer

I cracked the door to the bedroom open and entered the dimly lit room. A day earlier, my friend's husband, Breonus, had texted me: "We've called in hospice. You'd better come see Kisha as soon as you can." My beautiful friend, hairstylist, and former background singer had been in the fight of her life against breast cancer for a year and a half. Now with the palliative nurse on hand to make

Kisha more comfortable, it seemed she wasn't going to win the fight. I couldn't bring myself to believe it.

I had learned of her illness on a chilly January afternoon. Our scheduled hair appointment began as it had for over a decade. I sat in the salon chair with a towel and protective cape around my neck as Kisha worked her magic on my "new growth." The smell of chemical relaxer filled the air, and the sound of Wayne Brady giving away a vacation on *Let's Make a Deal* was drowned out by our conversation. Now that Kisha no longer traveled with me, we relished these hours when we could hash out the latest details of our days. I would catch her up on road life, the latest album I was recording, and any male suitors I had my eye on. She would talk about church, gush about Breonus or their son, BJ, and fill me in on her recent gigs.

That day, though, the appointment ended differently than past visits. She told her next client, who was already sitting in the extra chair in her room, that she needed an extra minute with me. She pulled me outside. Sensing that something was off, I furrowed my brow. "What's wrong?" I asked anxiously. I didn't expect Kisha's next words.

"I'm pregnant!" she said, flashing a beaming smile.

My jaw dropped and I squealed with excitement. BJ was about to turn ten, and Kisha was in her late thirties, so this news was an answer to my friend's prayers for another child. I had hundreds of questions, but they could wait. All I wanted was to celebrate with my friend and pray for the little baby growing inside. I laid my hand on her belly, ready to pray right then, but she stopped me before I could bow my head.

"Wait," she said in a way that made my stomach tighten. "There's something else I need you to pray for. I found a lump in my breast."

A few weeks later, Kisha received her official diagnosis of stage 3 breast cancer. When she called me with the news, I immediately went into fight-and-fix mode. I knew she had a battle in front of her, but she would get through this. I was 100 percent sure God would heal Kisha. Why wouldn't He? She had a young family that needed her. She was a bright light in so many lives. Countless people were praying in faith for her healing, and a full recovery would bring God so much glory.

Because she was pregnant, Kisha chose a less aggressive form of chemotherapy to protect her developing child. Her cancer was already advanced, but for Kisha, threatening the life of her baby wasn't even a choice. She would do whatever it took to keep him safe. And on June 8, 2013, Brennon Michael Mitchell was born perfect and healthy. When Kisha texted me the picture of her beautiful, chunky, chocolate baby, tears welled up in my eyes, and my heart rejoiced for my friend. I marveled at her grace and strength. Her top prayer request during her pregnancy had been for God to protect the child in her womb as she battled the disease threatening both of their lives. Brennon's birth was an incredible answer to prayer. And fresh hope rose in my heart. Now that Brennon had been born, Kisha could step up her cancer treatment. The worst was behind her, I thought.

SOUL SISTERS

I first met Lakisha Mitchell when I was a college student at Fisk University. I attended Greater Grace Temple Community Church where her husband was the pastor. At Greater Grace, as is the case in many Black churches, the pastor's wife is referred to as the First Lady. Just two years my senior, Kisha carried herself with grace and class beyond her years. She was always dressed to the nines, and she had the smoothest skin and whitest teeth I had ever seen. What impressed me the most about my First Lady, though, was her voice.

I'll never forget the first time I heard her sing. The choir stood as Kisha walked to the center of the stage, and the congregants shouted, "Sing, First Lady! Sing!" As the piano intro began, rowdy applause erupted along with voices calling out, "Oh, yes!" and "Come on, now!" The sanctuary quieted to a hush as Kisha's soulful voice launched into the first notes of "Fight On" by Kevin Davidson and the Voices.

My experience in church up to that point had taught me that singers onstage often employed showmanship and vocal acrobatics to hype up the crowd. While Kisha expertly handled the musical notes and had a voice that rivaled any singer I'd heard on gospel radio, there was something extra powerful behind her voice. As she belted the final lines of "Fight On," her song seemed to break chains and launch darts of hope into the congregation. Her worship felt like warfare—full of the grace and truth of Jesus—and she went to battle like no other I had ever witnessed.

When that woman worshipped, it was like Jesus was right there next to her. Everything else fell away as she brought those near her straight to the throne of God. From that point on, anytime Kisha stood on that stage, I braced myself for an encounter where heaven touched earth.

I held Kisha in such high esteem that I was somewhat surprised by how down-to-earth she was in person. During college I worked in the church office, and whenever Kisha came by, we had great conversations (just as we did later when I was seated in her stylist's chair). We could talk about everything from the sermon her husband had preached that week to the latest episode of *Oprah*. Our words flowed from the ridiculous to the holy and back again. She'd have me rolling in laughter one minute, then she'd be dropping a truth bomb the next.

One such bomb landed on me after one of our regular Wednesday night services. Kisha and I were walking to our cars when I noticed her eyeing my head. "Girl," she said. "What's going on with your hair?"

I laughed at her forthrightness and told her about the unfortunate experience I'd recently had at the salon across the street from Fisk. I didn't know why my hair was falling out, but Kisha—a practiced hairstylist— explained that the novice hairdresser I'd seen should have known better than to give me a relaxer *and* color at the same appointment. Hoping she could restore my hair back to health, I set up my first appointment with her and never looked back. (Now I understand why the salon across from Fisk was always empty and eventually closed down.)

My friendship with Kisha evolved over the years. After memorable moments at church, many days traveling on the road together, and hours seated in her salon chair, we developed a deep, unspoken love for each other. I say unspoken because neither of us really talked about it.

Both of us had experienced things in life that left us with hard shells that were not easy to penetrate. We were so similar in personality that when we argued, our stubbornness and quick wits translated to the effect of two championship boxers landing jabs in a ring. But when we finally calmed down enough to listen with the purpose of understanding, we would always find a way to unite and deepen our friendship.

VALLEY OF THE SHADOW OF DEATH

As I neared my friend's bed in June 2014, I hardly recognized her. Her skin sagged from all of the weight she'd lost, aging her decades. She couldn't speak, but she moaned softly.

"Can she hear me?" I asked Breonus.

"Yes, she can hear you," he said. "Talk to her."

Unsure of what to say, I sat down next to her bed, leaned in, and said, "Hey, Kish." She mumbled an unintelligible greeting. I awkwardly continued speaking to her as if we were just hanging out at her house on a normal afternoon. But I was painfully aware that this moment was *not* normal at all. Even holding her hand felt off. Under normal circumstances, Kisha and I *never* would have held hands. We often joked about how "anti–physical touch"

I was. (Kisha predicted this would change dramatically when I got married.) Part of me wondered if she felt it was strange to have her hand grasped in mine. Another part of me wondered if she could fully comprehend the moment or if she even recognized who I was. The whole situation felt surreal.

Breonus attempted to interpret her unintelligible sounds and finally suggested I sing to her. I nervously broke into the familiar hymn, "It Is Well with My Soul." To my surprise, Kisha began moaning along on pitch. Tears welled up in my eyes when we rounded the line, "Whatever my loss, Thou hast taught me to say, 'It is well, it is well with my soul.'" I wondered if that sentiment was true for Kisha. It certainly didn't feel true for me. My soul was not well. I was *not* okay with how my friend's journey had gone.

* * *

Ten months earlier, I'd pulled Kisha up onstage at a concert celebrating the release of my new album, *Overcomer*. At the time of Kisha's diagnosis, I had nearly completed the album, but we needed one more song. I told my producers and songwriters about Kisha, and the song

"Overcomer" was born with her in mind. None of us imagined how the anthem would strike a chord with listeners. It became a fight song for people all over the world going through battles of their own. The song gave them hope that with God's help they could prevail over hard circumstances in their lives.

That night, at the release concert, Kisha was caught off guard when I called her up to the stage. I told the audience that the song had been written for Kisha to encourage her in her fight. Just two months after she'd given birth to her son, my friend was the picture of health as she smiled shyly at my side.

"This is Kisha Mitchell, the overcomer in my life," I spoke into the microphone. "Kisha doesn't know this, but tonight we're raising $25,000 to cover her medical bills." The keyboard music swelled, and the crowd cheered. With my band and former background singers onstage surrounding her with love and support, we presented Kisha with a photo collage of pictures from our time touring together. The poster represented so many happy memories.

As Kisha studied the poster, she laughed at the picture of her, Laura, Myshel, and me standing in front of Niagara Falls—semistunned looks on our faces thanks to the strong wind and water pelting us from every side. I wondered if Kisha remembered how her comment about hoping her wig didn't fly off had made us all laugh the moment the photo was being snapped. I hoped that when she looked at the photos, she would be reminded of the army standing with her through every high and stormy gale.

I turned to Kisha and said, "We want you to know that we are fighting for you. We are *believing* for you. We are praying for you. And you're going to get through this thing. We're going to help you get through it." I believed every word. I imagined a glorious future moment when I would pull her up onstage at a concert again and declare that God had healed her completely.

Ten months later, as I looked at my friend's frail body lying in that bed, I tried to reconcile the reality of what I was seeing with my belief that God would still do a miracle. *He had to.* Kisha had a husband and two young sons who needed her. While I sat there by her bed, Kisha mumbled something I couldn't understand. Breonus leaned in, attempting to translate. He told me, "She says to keep praying . . . keep believing for a miracle." Even though the situation looked hopeless, I thought of the countless times in the Bible when God used a seemingly hopeless situation to display His glory and power to a watching world. I left that day choosing to believe that God would still save my friend's life.

SAYING GOODBYE

Three weeks later, I sat on a passenger van the day after a concert in Janesville, Wisconsin. It was Sunday, June 29, 2014, and our tour bus had broken down in the middle of the night on the way home to Nashville. We traded in our comfortable bunks, satellite TV, kitchenette, and bathroom, and boarded a cramped commuter van for the remaining seven-hour ride. With the rest of my band snoozing behind me as they leaned on guitar cases and amps, I stayed awake to keep my eye on the driver of the van. I suspected he was too tired to drive, because I had caught him nodding off when the van drifted into another lane. With my drooping eyes on alert, ready to yell the moment I sensed danger, my phone buzzed. I looked down at a text from Breonus, telling me that Kisha had passed away. I stared at my screen for a long time, trying to comprehend it. I didn't cry. I felt numb.

As the hours ticked by, I compartmentalized my emotions by fighting sleep and focusing on the drowsy driver who held our lives in his hands. When we pulled into a truck stop for a bathroom break, I told the band about

Kisha with very little emotion. I'm sure they offered their condolences, but in my shock at the time, their responses fell into a blurry mass of feelings I can't recall. To this day, all I remember from those moments is the gaping sense of loss that threatened to swallow me. *Kisha wasn't supposed to die. She was an overcomer. I prayed for her. I had faith. God didn't hold up His end of the bargain.*

With my devastation boxed up and shelved, the rest of the summer plodded on with contracts to fulfill and concerts to give. Barely having time to grieve my friend, I continued to perform at Christian music festivals in Dallas, Orlando, and other big cities. In the fall, I went on the Hits Deep Tour with TobyMac, Brandon Heath, Jamie Grace, and others. By then the song "Overcomer" was skyrocketing. It was played daily on Christian radio stations across the country and had even received a Grammy.

People came to my concerts to hear *that song*, but each performance threatened to pull out the pain from the box I had left on the shelf. Grief over my friend's death wasn't the only thing in that box; it also contained pain from past trauma, shame over my weight issues, and feelings of failure and inadequacy from being eliminated from *American Idol*. It seemed every grief or loss I'd suffered over the years was stuffed in that box, which was now threatening to overflow. As I sang the familiar words—"Whatever it is you may be going through, I know He's not gonna let it get the best of you"—I struggled to believe the sentiment was true. I found myself in a familiar place of disappointment and darkness and started to dread singing that song. Kisha hadn't overcome her battle, and I was beginning to feel like I wouldn't overcome my battle with doubt either.

WRESTLING WITH GOD

There's this wild Old Testament story in Genesis 32 where Jacob—one of the patriarchs of the Israelite people—wrestles with God. Crazy, right? He literally wrestles . . . with God. The backstory basically boils down to family drama: Jacob (with the help of his mom, Rebekah) steals his older brother Esau's birthright with a pot of soup. Their dad, Isaac, gives Jacob the blessing, and because that was a huge no-no, Jacob flees. Later he has to go back and face Esau, and let's just say he's not expecting a friendly reception.

The Bible says that Jacob, the night before going out to meet his brother, wrestles with a man all night. When the man sees he cannot overpower Jacob, the man touches Jacob's hip socket and wrenches it. At daybreak, the mystery man asks Jacob to let him depart, but Jacob replies, "Not . . . unless you bless me" (verse 26). You have to admire Jacob's boldness and grit.

The man says, "Your name will no longer be Jacob, but Israel, because you have struggled with God and with humans and have overcome" (Genesis 32:28). After that experience, Jacob walks with a limp. He *has* overcome, having received the blessing he desired. He becomes the father of God's chosen people but will forever carry the scar of the pain involved.

When Kisha died, I was angry. I felt betrayed by God. I had so much faith, and when the story didn't end the way I thought it should, I was mad. I wanted to give the Lord a piece of my mind. I wanted to shout, "You're just going to do what You want to do anyway, so leave me out of it!" Even now I still wrestle, like Jacob, wanting answers from the Lord. I still deeply feel the pain of losing my friend. Until I see Kisha in heaven, I will always limp from the loss.

When she first died, the pain felt unbearable. I wondered how a good God could allow this to happen. I'm a passionate person, and whether I'm cheering for my Tennessee Titans football team or praying for a sick friend, I'm *all in*. So as I was performing "Overcomer" in those months following Kisha's death, I began to think, *How can I get up on a stage and tell other people they can overcome, when I don't feel like I have?* At that point, I didn't think Kisha had overcome either. That was the start of going into the dark. As I pushed God away, retreated into myself, and embraced my go-to ways of coping (um, hello, food), I stepped out of the guiding light of my Savior and onto dangerous terrain. I wouldn't discover until several months later how truly dangerous that terrain had become.

Getting Real

- Kisha made an impact on my life through the kind of person she was and the way she worshipped. Who is a person who has greatly impacted your life?
- Did you ever pray big for something and receive "no" as an answer? How did you feel? How did it affect your relationship with God?
- When you're walking through difficult circumstances, what are your go-to ways of coping? How do these behaviors draw you closer to God or push you away from Him?
- The Bible says that Jacob wrestled with God and overcame. What does this passage tell you about what it means to be an overcomer?
- Have you ever been through something that caused you to "limp" like Jacob? What happened? How have you seen God at work in your limp?

· two ·

ONLY THE WORLD

'Cause it's only the world I'm living in
It's only today I've been given
There ain't no way I'm giving in
'Cause it's only the world
I know the best is still yet to come
'Cause even when my days in the world are done
There's gonna be so much more than only the world for me

A lot about my childhood was pretty average. I'm a "Cali-girl" born and raised in Citrus Heights, California, just outside Sacramento, where I lived with my mother, Ruby, and spent every other weekend with my dad and stepmom, John and Millie. Like many kids whose parents are divorced, I felt torn between my mom and my dad. I loved them both but struggled to express my loyalty when they were so divided. Furthermore, because my parents divorced when I was two and because my brother John lived with my dad, I struggled with feelings of rejection from my father. I knew he loved me—he told me so often—but in little Mandisa's mind, I felt like maybe I wasn't good enough, and that's why he left and chose not to be with me.

I learned to be alone at a young age. My mom worked full time, so during my school years, I spent a lot of time by myself. Every day I had a similar routine: come home from school, find a bag of chips or a box of cereal to snack on, and sit on the couch to watch TV. The snacking gave me something to do, but by late elementary school I started packing on the pounds. When something painful happened at school—whispered fat jokes, a bad grade, or anything else that made me uncomfortable—going home and getting lost in a TV show made me feel better. Food and TV were friends. I could escape the real world through the comedy, action, and drama of my favorite shows. I also dreamed about one day *being* on TV. My bathroom mirror transformed into a sold-out arena, my curling iron became my microphone, and the latest Whitney Houston cassette was the soundtrack to my award-winning performance.

When I was ten years old, my dad and stepmom moved to San Antonio, ending my twice-a-month visits. Up until then, I had been an active kid. In fact, I used to race the kids in my dad's neighborhood and win. I was fast! My brothers, John and Bryan, would have me race their friends, and those boys couldn't believe that this *girl* could beat them. My dad's departure to Texas only deepened the emotional wounds in my heart. I needed something to distract me from the pain, so "comfort food" lived up to its name. After Dad moved, and my brother John moved in with Mom and me, I really began to fill out. Overeating became a habit. No matter what emotion I was feeling, comfort could always be found in a box of donuts or a pint of ice cream.

Along with the extra weight I'd gained, I was also uncomfortable with my unique name: *Mandisa*. Mandisa means "sweet" in the language of the Xhosa, a South African people group. But my early experience with the name was anything but sweet; in fact, it was quite sour. My name was chronically mispronounced by students and teachers alike. Some bullies even nicknamed me "Medusa" (a figure in Greek mythology who turns people to stone and whose hair is made of venomous snakes). I came to see my unique name as a liability. In junior high, I asked my teachers to call me "Kandie," which concealed my real name from the other students. I went by this name all through high school.

God wasn't a big part of my life as a child. I did attend church with my dad and stepmom every other weekend before they moved, but it was more of a task to check off a to-do list. Because I wasn't a regular attender, I would often feel like an outsider around the other kids in Sunday school. Church became something I had to get through rather than a meaningful experience. I learned things *about* God, but I didn't have a relationship *with* God. I didn't recognize my sin or understand my need for a Savior. It was as if I were staring at a bunch of puzzle pieces and had no idea what the finished puzzle would look like. The things of God felt very distant from my everyday life.

As I hit my teen years, I struggled to fit in and find where I belonged. Growing up in the Sacramento Valley, I was literally a "valley girl" and had the speaking voice to go with it. I was one of only a few Black students at my high school. As a freshman, I hung out with a rough crowd. Some of those kids looked like me, and I longed to be accepted by them. But when they'd hear me talk, they'd say, "You talk like a white girl." Their negative judgments made me feel like I wasn't "Black enough" and needed to prove myself.

By age fourteen, I was headed down a dangerous path with the people I was allowing to influence me. During PE, I would go through lockers and steal money— behavior my "friends" seemed to celebrate. (It was also something that allowed me to buy sweets for my after-school treat.) I even tried smoking one day, but that experiment was short-lived. I still don't know how I was supposed to inhale, but I do know that when I breathed in the way my friend told me to, my throat burned so badly that I coughed all the way home. At home I soothed myself with a huge cup of orange juice paired with six waffles doused with butter and syrup. My friend could keep her cigarettes, but you'd better L'Eggo my Eggo.

My sophomore year of high school was pivotal for several reasons. I joined choir, which separated me from my former "friends," who accused me of thinking I was better than them. I was one of two Black students in the choir, but I felt like I'd found a home there. I had a great choir director, Mr. Robinson, who helped me expand my knowledge of music theory and improve my vocal performance. I'll never forget my audition for the California All-State Honor Choir, a competition for choral students throughout the state. Mr. Robinson had chosen the song "You'll Never Walk Alone" from the musical *Carousel*, for me to sing at the audition. As I listened to his recommendation, I thought it was perfect for me until I heard the soaring high note that was the pinnacle of the song. I was convinced I couldn't hit that note, but Mr. Robinson believed in me and taught me about diaphragm support and breath control. More than anything, he built my confidence. Not only did I make Honor Choir, but I also became a soloist in the final concert that year. I felt joy rehearsing and performing with my fellow "choir geeks," as we affectionately called each other. Music was my thing, and choir geeks were my people. I felt like I belonged.

I was also on the drill team that year. Even though I didn't look like the other girls on the team, learning the routines and dancing was fun and brought me joy. Our uniforms were a sleeveless top and short skirt, which looked cute on some of the girls but was not the most flattering look on me. One day, we performed a routine during a pep rally in the school gym. After we did a dance move where we jumped in the air and fell to the ground, I heard some students laughing from the bleachers. Later I found out that a student had made a wisecrack about the gym shaking when I dropped to the ground, causing those in earshot to erupt in laughter. Kids can be so mean. Over thirty years later, I still feel pain when I remember comments like those. Sticks and stones may break my bones, but words hurt in a different way. That day I ran to the bathroom and cried, before going home and downing almost an entire box of Honey Nut Cheerios.

Something else happened my sophomore year. In my creative writing class, I was assigned to read the novel *Stranger in a Strange Land* by Robert A. Heinlein. In the classic science fiction novel, the protagonist, Valentine Michael Smith, is a human born on Mars and raised by Martians. He comes to earth as a young adult, preaches love, establishes a church, and is ultimately killed by his enemies. Sound familiar? It's a classic messiah story. The story is pure science fiction, but it is also filled with spiritual symbolism, which raised my curiosity about God. The Holy Spirit was stirring in my heart.

I have noticed that God sometimes uses the most unusual things to draw people to Himself. I've heard of people coming to know Christ through random TV shows or secular college classes. Many of us can think of a moment or experience in our own lives where we can see God was pursuing or letting us know He was there. I sang about this in the song "God Speaking," which was on my first album, *True Beauty*. Here are some of the lyrics:

Have you ever heard a love song that set your spirit free?
Have you ever watched a sunrise and felt you could not
    breathe?
What if it's Him?
What if it's God speaking?

Have you ever cried a tear that you could not explain?
Have you ever met a stranger who already knew your
    name?
What if it's Him?
What if it's God speaking?

Who knows how He'll get a hold of us?
Get our attention to prove He's enough
He'll do and He'll use whatever He wants to
To tell us "I love you"

God was choosing small things and moments to reveal Himself to me. In John 6:44, Jesus says, "No one can come to me unless the Father who sent me draws them." The Father was drawing me to His Son, Jesus. The pieces didn't fit together yet, but everything in my life seemed to be pushing my thoughts toward heavenly things. For my birthday that year, I asked for a Bible. My friend Jennifer Bradshaw, who was a Christian, was excited to give me one and offered to answer any questions I might have. I had an ambitious plan to read the Bible cover to cover, but that plan fizzled somewhere around Leviticus. I didn't understand what I was reading, so I eventually set the Bible aside. Thankfully, God wasn't finished getting my attention.

SEARCHING FOR TRUE BEAUTY

That fall, when I had just turned sixteen, something terrible and transformative happened. My best friend's neighbor raped me. This boy was cute and funny, and even though I was overweight, he was interested in me. I enjoyed kissing him, but I certainly didn't want to have sex with him. As is the case for many young women, the rape wasn't a dramatic attack involving a weapon in a dark alley. He simply forced sex on me after I said no. The whole time it was happening, he kept telling me how beautiful I was. "You're so pretty. You're so pretty," he kept saying, but I kept saying no. I would later realize that this confusing set of events taught me to associate beauty with danger. I felt like my beauty had caused or invited the violation. This played into my food issues because I felt that if I gained a lot of weight and made my body unattractive, nothing like that could ever happen to me again.

After the rape, I felt so much shame. My thoughts accused me: *I should have screamed. I should have made him stop. Why did I let this happen?* At the core of it all, I believed my outward beauty was to blame. I felt like it was my fault, and I was too ashamed to tell anyone what had happened. Feelings of guilt and insecurity washed over me. My food issues spun out of control. I didn't ever want a repeat of what happened that day, so I put on even more weight in a subconscious attempt to protect myself. I quit the drill team, thinking maybe a cushion of fat would protect me from other pain. Even though I felt alone and believed I had to fix myself, God was still looking out for me and drawing me to Himself.

MEETING THE GREAT HEALER

That December my mom's coworker, Rebekah, invited us to go see the "Singing Christmas Tree" production at her church. Even though my new Bible had been gathering dust, my heart and mind continued to be drawn to spiritual things. At that Christmas production, God cracked my heart wide open. I sat fixated as the music and narration told the story of Jesus's life. From His birth to His humiliating death to His resurrection—I watched every scene with rapt attention, as if my life depended on it.

Eventually, the drama revealed the plan of salvation and the eternal life God offered through His Son, Jesus. Every nerve ending tingled as the scriptures penetrated my heart.

At the end of the production the pastor stood up and gave an invitation for anyone who wanted to give their life to Christ. He told the audience to close their eyes and bow their heads while he prayed a prayer we could repeat silently. As I thought about the guilt and shame I'd been carrying about my body and the rape, I felt the Holy Spirit burning a hole in my heart. Though I had heard the story of Jesus dying on the cross many times before, it was as if I had heard it with new ears. I finally understood that Jesus wanted to come into my life, free me from the weight of my shame, and make me a new creation. The best part was, He would do all the work. I wanted to respond! As the pastor prayed, I prayed with him. I told God that I knew I was a sinner and that I believed Jesus had died, risen again, paid the penalty for my sin, and given me eternal life. I told God I wanted to follow Him and allow Him to be the boss of my life from that day forward.

When the pastor said, "Amen," a sense of joy and peace washed over me. All those puzzle pieces seemed to fall into place, and I could see the beautiful picture of God's plan for me. The pastor's next words took me by surprise: "If you prayed that prayer, raise your hand." I froze. I was sitting right next to my mom and her coworker. I never expected to have to make my decision *public.* I slowly raised my right hand, the hand nearest the aisle, hoping my mom wouldn't notice. I wasn't sure what she would think about my profession. Ruby Berryman had been raised in church but rarely attended anymore, so we didn't discuss matters of faith.

As soon as I could, I lowered my hand. Then the pastor said, "Now if you've lifted your hand, come down here so we can meet you and give you some more information."

My chest tightened, and I hesitated. Mom may have missed my raised hand, but she would definitely notice if I left the pew. I don't know if it was the joy of my newfound salvation or boldness inspired by the Holy Spirit, but I felt myself standing from my seat and walking down the aisle to the pastor. There's something important about taking a public stand for Jesus. Once when Jesus was instructing His disciples, He said these sobering words: "Whoever acknowledges me before others, I will also acknowledge before my Father in heaven. But whoever disowns me before others, I will disown before my Father in heaven" (Matthew 10:32–33).

That may sound like a threat, but I think Jesus was simply talking about the natural allegiance that comes with a true decision to follow Him. We have to count the cost. Following Him isn't always easy or popular. It's not a 50/50 proposition, either, as in 50 percent my own life and desires, and 50 percent submitting to Jesus. He wants 100 percent. I have to be all in. And sometimes that means being public about my faith even when it's uncomfortable.

As we left the church that night, my mom was quiet. I think she realized I was on my own spiritual journey. I was so grateful that Rebekah had invited us to church. If she hadn't, I would not have heard the gospel at that time in my life when I needed Jesus so badly. I've thought about that experience many times since. Rebekah's relationship with my mom greatly impacted my life—and my mom's years later, when she made her own profession of faith. Relationships are so important when it comes to sharing Christ with others.

As a new believer, my life didn't change overnight. In fact, many aspects of it continued on pretty much the same at first. As a young Christian, I didn't yet know a lot of things about following Jesus. I knew I should be attending church, but my mom still didn't go and I didn't have a driver's license. Two years passed before I was able to go to church regularly. The first Sunday after I got my driver's license, I drove my mom's car to Genesis

Missionary Baptist Church. I knew of the church because of a Martin Luther King Jr. Day event I had sung at a few years earlier. (I may or may not have been influenced by their drummer, whom I met at that MLK event and had a huge crush on.)

At Genesis, I began to grow in my faith. I soaked up knowledge about God and the Bible like a sponge. I couldn't get enough. I never missed a Sunday or Wednesday night Bible study. I was hungry to learn more about God and what the Bible taught about how I should live.

NEW PATHS

When I graduated from high school, I enrolled at American River Junior College to study vocal performance. It was then that I decided to let go of my childhood nickname, "Kandie," and go by my given name, Mandisa. During my two years at American River, I thrived as part of the choral and jazz choirs. I learned about different techniques and styles as a soloist. Even though I'd found my place in the world of music and was starting to feel at home in my predominantly Black church, I longed to connect more with my African American roots. But how could I, this new believer, choir geek, California valley girl, really get in touch with her Black heritage? God already knew the path He had for me, and I never could have imagined how amazing it would be.

I love God's words in Isaiah 42:16, where He says, "I will lead the blind by ways they have not known, along unfamiliar paths I will guide them; I will turn the darkness into light before them and make the rough places smooth. These are the things I will do; I will not forsake them."

There are so many times in our lives when we cannot see the way forward. Maybe we don't know what job we're supposed to take or how to achieve a particular dream. The beautiful thing is, God knows all of that. I once heard someone say, "Do not fear tomorrow; God is already there." We don't have to be afraid when the path ahead is unclear, because God already knows what is coming and is at work making the rough places smooth.

One day I was talking to my guidance counselor at American River and said, "I want to go to a school with a predominantly Black student body and a good music program." I'm not even sure what caused me to say that. I think I wanted to feel like I fit in more with "my people." The counselor immediately suggested Fisk University in Nashville, Tennessee, home of the prestigious Fisk Jubilee Singers.

To understand the significance of this, you have to know a little more about Fisk. Fisk University opened in

1866, shortly after the end of the Civil War. The first university in America to provide a liberal arts education to "young men and women irrespective of color," Fisk is the oldest higher education institution in Nashville. The Fisk Jubilee Singers, an a cappella ensemble, started in 1871 to raise needed funds for the struggling university. Their name, "The Jubilee Singers," is a biblical reference to the Year of Jubilee written about in Leviticus 25. (Turns out I actually enjoyed that book of the Bible once I got through it.) Every fifty years there was to be a year when slaves were set free. The Jubilee Singers sang Negro spirituals originally sung by slaves prior to the Civil War. They performed for President Ulysses S. Grant, Mark Twain, and even Queen Victoria during an 1873 tour of Great Britain. The queen was so impressed with the Jubilee Singers that she said they must be from a "city of music," giving Nashville its nickname, "Music City."

Though they were often mistreated and rejected as they toured around US cities, the Fisk Jubilee Singers undoubtedly made a difference in race relations during the late 1800s. Their songs and performances began to change the attitudes of their predominately white audiences, and they regularly received standing ovations and praise.

Had I not felt the urge to attend a predominantly Black school, I would have missed the rich history and experiences awaiting me at Fisk. I applied to the illustrious university and was accepted. So in fall 1996, I moved halfway across the country to Tennessee, which felt a world away from California. I had no idea what to expect, but I fully believed God was directing my steps.

Getting Real

- Think of a time when you struggled to fit in. What happened? What did you learn through the experience?
- Sometimes experiences from our formative years shape us and influence our present struggles. What are some experiences from your past that affect you now?
- I came to know Christ when a friend invited my mom and me to church and I responded to the pastor's invitation. Describe your salvation experience. If you don't have one, what's holding you back? 2 Corinthians 6:2 says, "Now is the day of salvation." Think about how that truth applies to you.
- Read Matthew 10:32–33. What insight do you find in these verses? Have you ever had to take a public stand for Jesus? What happened?
- Has God ever led you on an unfamiliar path? How did you see God's provision through the experience?

three

GOOD MORNING

Wave away my yesterday
'Cause I'm leaving it behind me
Hello sunshine, come what may
I feel something new inside me
I hear the birds singing
Now my alarm's ringing
Get up, get up, hey!

It's a good morning
Wake up to a brand new day
(This morning) I'm step-stepping, stepping on my way
(Good morning) You give me strength, You give me just
   what I need
And I can feel the hope that's rising in me
Good morning

Moving halfway across the country to attend Fisk felt like relocating to a different planet. For one thing, I was surrounded by people who looked like me, which was a bit of a shock. Of the one thousand students at Fisk, you could count the number of white students on one hand. It was a total reversal from my experience in California. The other thing I quickly encountered when moving to Nashville was the culture shock of moving to the South. Although rich in African American influences (blues and jazz music, soul food, etc.), Nashville is also considered the buckle of the "Bible Belt," a region of the Southern US that is socially conservative, and where church attendance is higher than the national average. Where Sacramento was cool and relaxed, with a do-what-you-want vibe, in Nashville, cultural Christianity and church attendance was the norm. The friendliness also surprised me.

I remember walking down the street with a new friend shortly after I arrived at Fisk, and people were waving to us as we passed them. "Do you know all those people?" I asked my friend.

"No," she answered. "They're just being friendly."

"We don't do that in California," I told her.

In addition to the culture shock and the rigors of full-time college, I also had to deal with the challenges of living away from home for the first time. I was overwhelmed. As I looked at the unfamiliar sites around me, I even wondered if I'd made a mistake attempting such a drastic life change. Being in an environment where everyone looked like me was refreshing but also a little disconcerting. Everything felt so new and unfamiliar. I wanted to "be myself," but I wasn't sure who that was. The struggle to trade in Kandie, the California choir geek, for Mandisa, the Fisk Jubilee Singer, felt insurmountable. At first I was miserable. I remember calling my mom and friends back home every week and saying, "I can't stay here!"

That all changed when I got connected with the on-campus ministry of Bible Study Fellowship. This global ministry offers in-depth Bible studies in communities and on college campuses to help people pursue God and discuss His Word in community. We called our BSF group "YES ministries," which stood for "Young, Excited, and Saved." My friend Chandra Allen led weekly Bible studies on Monday nights.

As I began to study God's Word, my faith exploded. I was still homesick, but as I cried each night, thinking I just wanted to go home, I found myself talking to Jesus. My faith became real to me. It went beyond Sunday church experiences to something I depended on every day. I realized that being a Christian was about this amazing relationship I could have with God. As I studied, I began to see how incredible the Bible is. It isn't just some boring old history book about people who are nothing like me; it's the opposite. It's a picture of God's amazing heart for His children and His big, wonderful plan that stretches from Genesis to Revelation.

I had so many questions. And Chandra patiently answered them all. Ultimately, my transition to Fisk shook up my life in a very positive way. I was forced to wrestle with who I was (and wanted to be) and to make my faith my own. One of the studies I did with Chandra was *Experiencing God* by Henry and Richard Blackaby and Claude V. King. The study explored seven realities found in scripture that teach us how to have a true relationship with the Creator. For example, one of the realities is, "God is always at work around me." Another is, "I come to know God as I obey Him and He accomplishes His work through me." The study opened me up to a whole new understanding of God, the Bible, Jesus, the Holy Spirit, and other aspects of being a Christian. I realized the exciting adventure of following God with my whole heart as I surrendered my life to Him.

During my college years, God revealed to me the beauty of diversity and how He creates us all uniquely. I was learning a lot about myself—both as an African American woman and as a Christian. I had many things in common with my peers at Fisk, but I also had things in common with my "choir geek" friends in Sacramento. Most importantly, I had things in common with my brothers and sisters in Christ spread across the globe—the church. All of us have different gifts that God can use when we come together as one in love and service to Him. The apostle Paul talked about this in 1 Corinthians 12:12–14:

> Just as a body, though one, has many parts, but all its many parts form one body, so it is with Christ. For we were all baptized by one Spirit so as to form one body—whether Jews or Gentiles, slave or free—and we were all given the same Spirit to drink. Even so the body is not made up of one part but of many.

I think we forget that God's body, the church, has many parts. We're not all meant to look and act and think exactly the same. God demonstrates His glory through diversity and the different gifts and personalities of His followers. During college, I was the president of the Black Mass Gospel Choir. Chandra led Bible studies. Our roles and responsibilities looked different, but we were both using the gifts God had given us to further His kingdom. At times in my life, I have wanted to be like someone else. I've looked at someone else's gifts or position or appearance and wished I were like them. But God designed us each unique, like a fingerprint, with specific good works that only we can accomplish.

Ephesians 2:10 says, "For we are God's handiwork, created in Christ Jesus to do good works, which God prepared in advance for us to do." The word *handiwork* in that verse is translated from the Greek word *poiema*, which is the word from which we derive our English word *poem*. You and I are a *poem*—an artistic work—created by God. Our details and quirks are not inconsequential. God has a purpose for each and every one, namely good works—actions that help others and bring glory to the Father.

Along with beginning to understand my identity in Christ at Fisk, I also realized some things about my identity as a Black woman. I attended Greater Grace Temple Community Church, where I met Breonus Mitchell, my pastor, and Kisha, my "First Lady." At Greater Grace, my faith deepened. The way Pastor Mitchell preached made the Bible come alive for me. I could read the few short chapters in Joshua about the Israelites' time in Gilgal, but I had no idea how it applied to my life until Pastor Mitchell's four-part series on the passage.

And the music! You haven't lived until you've heard a Black church choir break out into song. You can trace the celebratory roots of Black culture all the way back to Africa. The clapping, dancing, and shouting would best be described as a "praise party." The people of Greater Grace fervently invited the Holy Spirit into their midst. I loved worshipping God in this way and found true community at church.

As I studied the history of African Americans at Fisk, I not only gained a rich sense of my heritage, but I also realized being Black is way more than talking a certain way, dressing a certain way, or listening to a certain kind of music. God was saying, "This is how I made you. I gave you your 'valley girl' speaking voice. I gave you your wide vibrato and soulful singing voice. I gave you your skin color. I made you exactly how I wanted you to be."

Growing up, I had felt like everything associated with the word *black* was bad—black holes, black sheep, black as night, etc. White was always associated with purity and light. Subtle things I'd picked up during my childhood reinforced the idea that black is bad and white is good. Fisk helped me realize that black is good too. Though I still had a journey of self-acceptance ahead of me—such as making peace with my hair—for the first time in my life, I was truly proud to be a Black woman.

LIFE OF MINISTRY

When I graduated from Fisk, I had no idea what to do next. My major in vocal performance didn't exactly set me up to enter the job market, and I quickly learned that crashing on Chandra's couch without a job could only last for so long. Since I was seeking God's will, I decided to go through the *Experiencing God* Bible study again. After all, the subtitle is "Knowing and Doing the Will of God." One day, after I had finished the study for that day, I turned over the book and a single word caught my eye: *Lifeway.* I noticed that the publisher's corporate office was located in Nashville. *Maybe I could get a job there,* I thought.

The next day I looked on the website and scoured the job postings. I saw a job opening in the music department and felt sure it was meant to be. It wasn't. I didn't get that job, but I was hired on in customer service. Lifeway produced Sunday school curriculum, and my job was to type in orders mailed in from churches. It wasn't glamorous, but it paid the bills.

Each day, as I entered Sunday school orders from around the country, I would listen to music in my headphones and sing. I guess I was singing louder than I thought, because people heard me. A few told me I should join the employee choir. You already know how I feel about choir, so I did exactly that. The choir performed at the organization's chapel services, and each year, the company put on a big Christmas show. I was asked to sing a solo in that, and before I knew it, people knew me as the girl in customer service who sings.

In spring 2001, Lifeway put together a three-day "Spring Revival" event that featured worship leaders and Christian speakers. Travis Cottrell was one of the worship leaders who came to minister at that event. He leads worship for Living Proof Live conferences, part of the ministry of Bible teacher Beth Moore. I had done Beth's *Breaking Free* Bible study during college, but I didn't know anything else about her ministry. I was recruited to be part of Travis's worship team for the revival. The first time I met Travis, our team practiced the beautiful song "Come, Ye Sinners, Poor and Needy." I wasn't familiar with the old hymn, but Travis put a funky, contemporary beat to it, so it was love at first sing.

"That song is a jam!" I said. "It's so fun. Did you write it?" Travis looked at me with amused shock.

"You don't know 'Come, Ye Sinners, Poor and Needy'?" he said. "Are you sure you're saved?" We both laughed.

That was my first dose of Travis. He's a close friend to this day. On the last day of the event, Travis brought his regular praise team from Living Proof Live. Tammy Jensen, who would later become one of my best friends, was on that praise team. I remember seeing her on that stage worshipping so freely with her hands straight up in the air . . . among Southern Baptists. It was not something I was used to seeing at Lifeway, but I saw Tammy and thought, *I want to worship like that.* It was more than just her physical posture. She worshipped as if it were just her and Jesus alone, intimate and personal.

Before Travis left, he told me, "Hey, I'd love to have you at one of our Beth Moore events some time. Give me your number." Thinking he was just being nice, I told him he could call me at Lifeway.

A few months later, a coworker and I decided on our own to drive to Memphis and attend a Beth Moore Living Proof Live event. The teaching and the worship were incredible, and before long, I began dreaming about singing and leading worship with the Living Proof Live team. During a break, I saw Travis walking past the stage. I didn't think he'd remember me, but when I approached him, he said, "Mandisa! I've been thinking about you! I really want to get you singing at one of these."

Two weeks later, while in the call center at Lifeway typing in orders, a coworker handed me a message informing me of a missed call from Travis Cottrell. I nervously called him on my break and found out he needed a female vocalist last-minute to fill in for the biggest Living Proof Live event of the year. It would be held that weekend in Charlotte, North Carolina. I would have to learn thirty songs in three days.

"Will you do it?" he asked.

My first thought was not about learning that much music so quickly. My concern was that I couldn't afford the flight. I wondered if I had some airline miles I could use to purchase it. After I expressed my worry, Travis had a hard time holding back his laughter. He explained that they would pay for my travel and also pay me as a musician. It somehow didn't occur to me that this opportunity was a job. I felt so honored to be asked and quickly agreed to the gig.

Over the next three days, I crammed to learn thirty songs (including the sign language to go with the hymn "It Is Well with My Soul"). I felt like I was back in school studying for a big test. On Friday night I stood with the rest of the worship team on a round stage in the middle of a huge arena filled with twenty thousand excited women. Flashes of my bathroom mirror swirled through my mind as I held the microphone—no longer the curling iron—shaking in my hand. The countdown began, and I listened for the band to kick in with the energetic beat of our first song. The deep pounding in my ear was not the kick drum, but my erratic heart racing with nerves. As the lights went down, the ladies in the audience whistled and screamed with anticipation. Travis leaned over and said, "Sing 'Amazing Grace.'"

"What?" I asked incredulously.

"Let's start with you singing 'Amazing Grace'—a capella—right now." His entire face lit up like it was the most inspired idea of all time. That's Travis—impulsive, spirit-led, nerve-racking Travis. I had never been so flustered in all my life. Voice trembling, body quivering, but spirit soaring, I opened my mouth and let the familiar refrain wash over me.

> Amazing grace
> How sweet the sound
> That saved a wretch like me
> I once was lost
> But now I'm found
> Was blind but now I see

The deafening applause that followed my solo mingled with the band kicking in with the pulsating beat of Travis's arrangement of "All Hail the Power of Jesus' Name." That unforgettable weekend would be the first of many as I became a regular singer for the Living Proof Live worship team. I blossomed under Travis's leadership. He has an amazing worshipper's heart and a way of blending the old with the new. He would take a song that had been important to Christian worship for centuries and add a contemporary twist to help it reach a new generation. Because of Travis I came to know and love hymns. He would combine them with contemporary worship songs, including some of the gospel songs I would hear at Greater Grace. This diversity of music influenced me greatly.

I was also tremendously impacted by Beth. I have never met anyone so in love with the Word of God as Beth Moore. Her love of the Bible was infectious. So many of her teachings will stick with me for the rest of my life. I will never forget a message where she talked about bitterness. She quoted Hebrews 12:15, which says, "Look after each other so that none of you fails to receive the grace of God. Watch out that no poisonous root of bitterness grows up to trouble you, corrupting many" (NLT).

She went on to talk about Naomi from the book of Ruth. Naomi had lost her husband and her sons. In those times, a widow had no resources or respect without a husband or children. She and her daughter-in-law Ruth traveled from Moab back to the town of Bethlehem, where they arrived penniless and pitiable. Naomi was so distraught that she declared, "Don't call me Naomi . . . Call me Mara, because the Almighty has made my life very bitter" (Ruth 1:20). Naomi's words may be relatable to some of us, but Beth pointed out the power of Naomi declaring that over herself. She chose to call herself by the name of something destructive and counter to God's will for her life.

How many times do we do the same? The things I declare about God and myself have power. My perspective shapes my worship, and it shapes the kind of Jesus-follower I am. Psalm 89:2 says, "I will declare that your love stands firm forever, that you have established your faithfulness in heaven itself." That's just one example. The Psalms talk about declaring His marvelous deeds, His praise, His name, and His glory. When I regularly declare truths about God, my own struggles fade into the background. Instead of calling myself names and giving in to bitterness, I can accept what God says about me—that I am His beloved child, that He has created me for good works, that I am never alone or abandoned.

Beth's teaching helped me see that God's Word is rich and full, and I could spend a lifetime trying to soak up all its wonders and never even scratch the surface. During the nearly five years I toured with Travis and Beth, my faith grew tremendously. I was blessed with laughter and community and camaraderie. Those times together shaped me and prepared me for the ministry God would eventually call me into.

Beth told me a story about the first time she knew God was calling me into public ministry. At the Living Proof Live events, I always sang with the team. But at one event, Travis asked me to share before we sang. Beth said, "When I saw you exhorting in the Word of God, I knew our time with you was short." At that time, I had no idea how much standing on a stage and talking about God would be part of my future. But Beth saw it. Sometimes you don't see things in yourself, but others can call out those qualities in you. That is what Travis and Beth did for me, and I'm so very grateful.

My last event was in Fresno, California, in December 2005. I walked off that stage and flew straight to Hollywood for the semifinals of *American Idol*. On that day, how would I have known what the future would hold? But God certainly knew.

In fact, God already knows all the details about our lives. He knows what we will do. He knows whom we will meet along the way. He even knows the very day we will die. As we follow Him, He orchestrates the details of our lives to allow us to walk out the purposes He has planned for us. Let's think about it: What gave this average California girl the desire and courage to move to Nashville to attend a historically Black college? Why did she randomly see the word *Lifeway* on the back of a book and think to look for a job there? And why, at an entry-level data entry job, did this woman get *discovered* as "the girl who sings" and over time meet some amazing ministry leaders because of it? God made all of these things happen. I have no doubt about that. God knew the lessons I needed to learn, and the ways I needed to be humbled. But He also knew exactly where I needed to be. So far, God had provided for me in big ways. But the next part of the journey would be the bumpiest and most intense yet.

Getting Real

- Think of a time when you went through a major change or transition. What happened, and what did you learn through it?

- Name a time in your life when you experienced massive spiritual growth. What factors led to this experience?
- When I graduated from college and didn't have a job, I happened to see the name of my future employer on the back of a Bible study resource. Have you ever experienced God speaking to you in an unusual or unexpected way? What happened?
- Travis Cottrell and Beth Moore had a big influence on my spiritual life. Name someone who has had a big effect on your spiritual life and what you learned from that person.
- Read Proverbs 16:9. Talk about a time when you were very aware that God was establishing your steps.

· four ·

THE ONE HE
SPEAKS THROUGH

He might use your words to heal a heart that has been
   bruised
He might use your hands to rescue
He might use your whisper, or maybe your smile
To tell somebody that they're worthwhile
You might be the one He speaks through
The one He speaks through

When *American Idol* premiered in summer 2002, it quickly became must-see TV for me. If I wasn't in a living room watching episodes with a group of friends, I was calling and texting with them, comparing notes on each superstar hopeful. The moment the show's host, Ryan Seacrest, announced that phone lines were open, the next two hours were spent speed-dialing votes in for my favorite contestants.

In the back of my mind, I always wondered what my chances would be in front of sweet Paula Abdul; the dawg, Randy Jackson; and the infamous Simon Cowell. While many viewers enjoyed the cutting jabs that Simon would make during the auditions, I always felt bad for the contestants on the receiving end. I shuddered to imagine the embarrassment that would come with being ridiculed on national television. Because the age limit was twenty-four, and I was a few years past that, I didn't have to worry about it. That was until season four, when they officially raised the contestant age limit from twenty-four to twenty-eight.

While multiple friends implored me to audition, my fear kept me safely watching the highs and lows of others from the comfort of my couch. But as auditions for season five approached (along with my twenty-ninth birthday), I knew it would be my last chance to audition for my all-time favorite show. When I was an old woman, I didn't want to look back on this time and wonder what could have happened if I'd taken the leap.

As I watched the season-four *American Idol* finale featuring Carrie Underwood and Bo Bice, I made the decision to step out of my comfort zone and audition. I found a regional audition three hours away in Memphis, but a few weeks later Hurricane Katrina pummeled the Gulf Coast and the auditions were cancelled. I had been asking God to make it clear if I was supposed to audition for season five, so I took it as a sign. Years of insecurity over comments others had made about my weight made it easy to let go of an opportunity that could throw me into the path of Simon Cowell. I was actually a bit relieved that it didn't seem to be God's plan for me after all.

But a few weeks later I was surfing the internet and discovered the "Atlanta Idol" audition put on by Atlanta's Star 94 FM pop radio station. The winner would receive airfare for two to the Chicago auditions, an overnight stay in a hotel, and priority access to the front of the audition line. *Maybe one last crack at it wouldn't hurt,* I thought. After all, all I had to do was call a phone number and submit a sixty-second recording of my voice. The song "Rock Steady" by Aretha Franklin had been stuck in my mind after hearing it in a movie that week, so I spent an hour rehearsing it in my bedroom to ensure that it showed off my range and personality. I called the number, stated my name and phone number, and launched into what I hoped would be a memorable performance that would grab the attention of whatever intern they had sifting through the many recordings. I had one shot. Twenty seconds into my recording, just as I was about to soar into the high notes that I hoped would set me apart, the phone line suddenly went dead. *Arggghhh!*

It seemed my *Idol* dream was also dead. That was it. No more attempts for me. So you can imagine my surprise three days later when the station called to let me know I was one of six finalists. I informed the woman on the phone that I lived in Nashville, but she told me that so long as I could report to the studio in Atlanta first thing Friday morning (two days later), I was good to go. I quickly hatched a plan to drive to Atlanta on Thursday night and stay with my college roommate, Pam, who lived near the city. Pam was the only person I told. That way, I reasoned, when I was eliminated, I would save myself the embarrassment of letting everyone down.

The night before the contest, after driving the 250 miles to Pam's house, I couldn't sleep. After tossing and turning for several hours, I finally got up around 3:45 a.m. and started getting ready. I had to report to the station at seven a.m. As I drove to the studio, I felt on edge—both from having to navigate the traffic and from the little voice inside telling me I wasn't good enough. Those feelings were confirmed when I saw the other five finalists. They were hip and young and looked like models. Many of them, high school and college students, came with their parents. As we sat together in the kitchen of the radio station and tried to make conversation, I felt a familiar emotion: I was out of place.

I wonder if Jesus ever felt out of place. I think Isaiah 53:2 gives us some insight: "He grew up before him like a tender shoot, and like a root out of dry ground. He had no beauty or majesty to attract us to him, nothing in his appearance that we should desire him." I find it interesting that the Bible talks about the Messiah's physical appearance. When I think of the depictions of Jesus I have seen in movies and television shows, this description in Isaiah does not fit. People were drawn to Him—attracted to Him—but for a deeper reason than His appearance. Jesus certainly knew how it felt to be overlooked and even ridiculed—a few of my biggest fears.

As I sat in that kitchen, feeling insecure about my outward appearance, I wondered if I'd made a mistake in coming. When it was my turn to sing, there was no phone line to cut me off. I belted my sixty seconds of "Rock Steady," and after I finished, the judges were silent. Finally, one of them spoke: "You definitely would have made it if you'd auditioned in Memphis. Amazing voice!" The judges deliberated for a few minutes then announced me as their choice for "Atlanta Idol." The judges explained that their selection was "all about the voice." I'm sure they meant it as a compliment, but it reminded me that at my weight, I still didn't fit the image of what an American Idol should look like.

THE BIG AUDITION

Three days after my "Atlanta Idol" win, I flew to Chicago and checked into my hotel to prepare for the biggest audition of my life. Pam, who had been ecstatic but not surprised by my win, used the other ticket I'd won to fly in from Atlanta and be with me through the experience. While thousands of *Idol* hopefuls camped out in sleeping bags at Soldier Field for a chance to audition the following morning, Pam and I enjoyed the swanky accommodations at the Hyatt Regency. That night I spent time reading my Bible, praying, and journaling. I felt unsure of God's exact plan, but I knew He was with me.

Audition day, September 16, dawned cold and rainy. I hadn't thought to bring an umbrella, so my curls drooped along with my spirits. Pam and I arrived at Soldier Field around six a.m., joining some fifteen thousand *Idol* hopefuls. I walked to the bleachers set aside for contest winners. I remember feeling starstruck when I saw season-three *Idol* greats Jennifer Hudson and George Huff walk by. Would I make it as far as they had?

At nine a.m. Pam was whisked away to the guest area, while I was ushered into a large tent set up on the field. Contest winners would get to audition first. We had been told to prepare two songs and be ready to sing a third, chosen by producers. My group of four was sent to a tent to sing for an assistant producer. A Black woman who appeared to be in her thirties looked up from behind a table. I felt like we could be friends, but in that moment, it was all business. She sternly instructed us to sing our prepared songs. She would stop us when she'd heard enough, she said.

After stopping the first two contestants midsong, she asked them to prepare their second selections. I was up next. I belted out "Rock Steady," snapping my fingers and shaking my hips. "Step back, please," she said when I'd finished my segment. I didn't know if that was good or bad. While each of the other three contestants sang a second song, I waited, doubt creeping in. Once again, I was the odd man out.

I was shocked when the woman told the other contestants they had been cut. She turned to me and smiled. "You'll be moving on," she said. "Go up the stairs to the Cadillac Club to wait for your audition with Ken and Nigel." I knew Ken Warwick and Nigel Lythgoe as the executive producers of *American Idol*. A little while later, with my confidence rising, I walked into the room filled with rolling cameras and began to sing "Rock Steady." A few bars in, that rising hope plummeted when Ken stopped me abruptly.

"Can you sing something more current?" he asked. My brain reeled, trying to come up with something on the spot.

Nigel spoke up. "Do you know any Janet Jackson or Alicia Keys?"

Caught a bit off guard, I said, "I can sing 'Fallin.'" I got out two lines of the Alicia Keys hit before they stopped me. I would later discover that they couldn't get copyright clearance for "Rock Steady," so the show would edit in this short moment of "Fallin'" as if I had sung it before the judges. That's television magic.

The executive producers began discussing my performance as if I weren't in the room. I listened in tense silence as Ken said something about my "gospel diva" vibe being overdone and boring. *Yikes.*

Then I heard Nigel say, "It's a definite *yes* for me."

"Am I in?" I didn't mean to speak the words out loud, but they rushed out before I could stop them.

"Congratulations," Nigel said. I left the room screaming with my yellow ticket as cameras zoomed in to catch my reaction. I would be singing in front of Randy, Paula, and Simon . . . but not until four days later. When I first heard this piece of news, I panicked. The "Atlanta Idol" contest had only put me up at the hotel for one night. Where would I stay for four days? I remembered my college friend Chandra had a cousin in Chicago, and after a few phone calls, Alberta graciously offered to take me in. I spent the time working up some more modern songs and doing laundry, since I had only packed for one night.

A few days later I reported to the W Hotel in downtown Chicago. Of the fifteen thousand people who had auditioned four days earlier, only 250 had made it to this round. The judges would hear 125 singers each day. As we waited in a line wrapped around the outside of the hotel for what would come next, we must have been a sight to behold. Some contestants had dressed in wacky costumes to catch the judges' attention. One young woman wore a prom dress and kept saying she was going to ask Ryan Seacrest to prom. A man with hairy legs was dressed as Dorothy from *The Wizard of Oz*. And another guy was dressed as the Statue of Liberty. I wore a flowy black blouse with a chiffon fringe overlay, jeans, and a pair of heeled sandals. I remember shivering as wind blew off Lake Michigan and right through my lightweight clothing.

Once inside, the other contestants and I were led into a large room where we would wait for our turn to sing.

Those five hours felt like fifty as the sounds of crying and cheering rang through the hallways. Finally, it was my turn to perform for the judges. I walked with my head held high into the room and flashed a brilliant smile, hoping to mask my lack of confidence. You would think that singing in front of thousands of women could have prepared me for this moment, but the ladies at the Living Proof Live events were always smiling back. Simon Cowell was not. I didn't know what the outcome would be. I just hoped to get out of it unscathed by Simon's sharp tongue.

When Randy asked me my name, I answered, "Mandisa."

"Mandisa what?" he asked.

"Just Mandisa," I said. "The first name is enough to deal with, I think."

I put my performance chops to work on "Rock Steady" one last time. When I was finished, Paula said, "Whew! You had Simon rockin'!" Randy's accolades included a couple of "yos" and "dawgs," but Simon's words meant the most. He said, "Terrific—everything I hoped you would be." He continued in that British accent, telling me that I had a great voice and a pretty face. Where I expected ridicule, I received only praise. When the judges unanimously voted me through to the Hollywood round, I screamed in excitement. As I left the room, waving my "golden ticket," Ryan Seacrest and the camera crew were waiting.

"How do you feel?" Ryan asked.

"This feels like heaven!" I said.

YOU'RE GOING TO HOLLYWOOD

The next two months were a whirlwind. I had gotten through the audition process in one piece, but having never missed an episode of *American Idol*, I knew the next round was brutal: Hollywood week.

While my worst nightmare of Simon making fun of my weight had not come true, I was determined to spend the rest of September, October, and November crash-dieting to get off as much weight as I could. If the camera added ten pounds to one's appearance, I wanted to take off at least twenty. Carrot juice, salads, and hours on the treadmill became regular staples for me that fall.

I went into this journey simply wanting no regrets. After having made it so far, I wondered, *Do I actually have a shot?* I tried to quell my optimism, expecting the bottom to drop out at any moment, but I found myself daydreaming of possibilities.

I held my tongue about the exciting events in Chicago for as long as I could, especially because the nondisclosure agreement I signed in Chicago forbade me from telling anyone about my experience until the show's premiere in January. I technically didn't confirm my "so-far-so-good" *Idol* journey to my friends on the Living Proof Live team at my last event in Fresno, California, in December. However, when they saw that I was flying to Los Angeles after the weekend and not back home to Nashville, they put two and two together.

God used that last event with Beth, Travis, and the team to prepare me spiritually for the week ahead. Beth taught from Psalm 40 about the Lord helping us and guiding our steps. Psalm 40:3 resonated with me: "He put a new song in my mouth, a hymn of praise to our God. Many will see and fear the LORD and put their trust in him." That was my desire. I wanted others to see the Lord through me. I wanted Him to use my words and my song to bring hope and healing to others. I even put together a few "spiritual survival kits" to hand out to fellow contestants once I arrived. In each bag, I placed a devotional booklet I'd written to focus our minds on things above, along with a pocket-sized Bible and some other goodies. I prayed that God would show me the people who needed the spiritual encouragement. I quickly found three young women—two I met at the airport and one whom I had heard was a Christian—to give the bags to. They thanked me, and one girl even cried when she received it. I love the body of Christ. There is a fellowship among us that causes strangers to feel like sisters and brothers. Even while competing with one another, the prayers and encouragement I shared with those three ladies that week was a lifeline.

Because I was an *Idol* fan, I kind of knew what to expect going into Hollywood week. At our first meeting, a producer warned us this would be the hardest week of our lives. He told us our group of 165 would be divided. On the first day, half of us would audition, singing a song we'd selected from a list of twelve, while the other half would go on a tour of Hollywood. On day two, the groups would switch.

On my first day, I was part of the tour group. We rode a double-decker bus, toured the famous Hollywood Bowl music venue, and traipsed along the Hollywood Walk of Fame with its brass stars containing the names of movie and music royalty. We ended our day at the Santa Monica Pier, where we gazed at the Pacific Ocean. A few people even walked into the surf, fully clothed. I simply took it in from the safety of the sand. There is something about the vastness of an ocean that makes me appreciate the omnipotence of God. Seeing as far as the eye can see, yet knowing it doesn't even scratch the surface of the enormity of God's power and presence, always causes my heart to reflect. I have read Psalm 139:17–18 countless times. My mind knows that God's thoughts about me are precious and outnumber the grains of sand. But in that moment, actually standing with my toes *in* an unfathomable number of grains of sand, a new understanding of His love for me, and the assurance of His plans for me, stirred my heart with awe.

The next day I put on a flowy turquoise blouse and sleek black pants. I twisted my hair into an updo and secured it with a barrette. I was hatching a plan to make my performance stand out. We auditioned by rows, this time with a piano and background vocals. I sang the Donna Summer classic "Dim All the Lights." The first part of the song is slow and soulful. Then the song suddenly switches to an upbeat tempo. At that point in the song, I strategically pulled the barrette from my hair and shook out my silky black locks. I shimmied across the stage, putting my all into my performance. The audience of my fellow contestants jumped to their feet cheering me on. After everyone in my row had performed, the judges asked a few of us to step forward. I was through to the next round.

With ninety-nine contestants remaining, the next part of the competition involved splitting into groups of three or four to perform one of five preselected songs. I teamed up with three other girls—Lauren, Veronica, and Elease. We called ourselves "Reziliance." We chose "Band of Gold" as our song and stayed up until three a.m. practicing our harmonies and dance moves. After an hour of sleep back at the hotel, I rejoined the girls to rehearse until it was our turn to perform for the judges. Although we performed well together, I was the only one of my group to advance.

The sixty-six remaining contestants would sing one more a capella song. Unlike previous rounds, where the judges' comments would reveal how they felt about your performance, this time we would sing our song and walk off the stage without any feedback whatsoever. I sang "Something to Talk About" by Bonnie Raitt. I knew the chorus would really showcase my range, but the lack of sleep was catching up with me. I blanked on some of my words, and Simon abruptly raised his hand, commanding me to stop before the chorus. I left the stage embarrassed and ashamed that I'd botched my performance. On the bus ride back to the hotel, I was in a daze. I had come so far and sensed I was at the end of the road. With disappointment trying to overtake me, I slipped in my earbuds and listened to worship music. CeCe Winans's soulful voice assured me that God's strength is perfect when my strength is gone. I felt weak, but I was reminded once again that the Lord was strong, and He was directing my steps.

Back at the hotel we were divided into four groups and placed in separate conference rooms. I knew from the past season that the judges usually dismissed two rooms and accepted two. I had been preparing my heart to go home, but looking around at the people in my room, I felt some hope. Many of them had given strong performances. I stood at the back of the room when the judges finally entered. At first they just stared at us, prolonging the suspense. Finally, Simon spoke: "Should I just get on with it? . . . This group has made it through to the next round." I stood in disbelief as the others cheered and began to embrace. I had survived yet again. But the hardest part of this journey was still yet to come.

PAIN ON DISPLAY

After Hollywood week, we all went home and back to our regular lives. That was one of the strangest Christmas seasons ever. As I celebrated the birth of my Savior, like Mary, I was treasuring something in my heart: the fact that I had been *chosen*. I knew there was no guarantee I would sing in the semifinals. Over the next month the judges would review our performances and cut the remaining

Idol contestants down from forty-four to twenty-four—twelve men and twelve women. But even if I didn't make the cut, I had so much to celebrate. I believed God had truly used me to be a light on the show and to my fellow contestants. Not only that, but the judges liked me and respected my talent.

Leading up to the premiere of *American Idol* season five, commercials revealed that Chicago would be featured on the first episode. One such advertisement showed me bursting through the door screaming and waving my golden ticket to Hollywood. The cat was officially out of the bag. So on January 16, 2006, my friends Chance and Jennifer Scroggins hosted an *American Idol* premiere party. When I showed up to their house, I was touched to see that they wore custom-made T-shirts proclaiming: "Mandisa is my American Idol—All Hail the Diva." With more than twenty of my friends in attendance, my heart was full of anticipation to share my *Idol* success with them. They peppered me with questions about what happened behind the scenes. What was Ryan Seacrest really like? Was there anyone I felt sure would make it far? Was there any drama between other contestants? Chance set the show to record while we enjoyed some snacks and I shared as many stories as I could. We planned to start watching a little late so we could fast-forward through the commercials.

Finally, it was time to watch. We laughed at the ridiculous auditions and talked excitedly about the showstoppers, pausing the TiVo while I shared insight about fellow contestants and audition moments. I couldn't wait for them to watch *my* audition, where even grouchy Simon had given me kudos. Before my audition played, the phone rang. Chance took the call in another room. Soon he returned and beckoned me to come over. I could see the concern in his eyes. He lowered his voice as he told me that Travis was watching the show in real time. "After you left the room, Simon made rude comments about your weight," he said.

My mouth went dry, and I felt the blood drain from my face. This was my worst nightmare, and unexpected because of the kind things Simon had said in the room. Not only was it happening in front of thirty million TV viewers, but it was about to be broadcast in front of some of my closest friends. Despite the dread I felt at the thought of my friends witnessing my public humiliation, I decided to stay. Excited squeals rang out as my face appeared on screen, then a hush fell over the room. This was the moment we had all been waiting for, but knowing what was coming dampened the thrill of the moment for me. My friends cheered as I sang my song and the judges offered their compliments. They watched as I danced out of that audition room in excitement. Then the camera zoomed back to the judges' table, and Simon uttered one of his famous digs. "Do we have a bigger stage this year?" he asked, referring to my size.

Paula gave him a backhanded slap and told him she thought I had a "Frenchie thing" going on (referring to former contestant Frenchie Davis's powerful voice).

"Forget Frenchie," he quipped. "She's like *France*."

My friends went silent, and all eyes turned to me. I shrank under their pitying gazes. "It's okay," I said. "I'm okay." But I wasn't. And they knew it.

Sometimes community can be uncomfortable. I consider myself an ambivert, a combination of an introvert and an extrovert. There are times when I am energized by being with people, and there are times when my tank is filled by time alone. In that moment, I longed for the latter. When I experience pain, I like to retreat. I isolate (and eat) until I am numb. In this case, I had to feel pain, real time, under the compassionate gazes of my friends. It felt terribly uncomfortable.

"Simon's a jerk," one of them said. Another swooped in to give me a hug. I accepted their kind words, but inwardly I longed to run away and hide. The mood in the room had shifted. When the show was over, my girlfriends Fiona, Tammy, and Alicia took me aside to pray for me. They prayed for God's closeness to be felt by my broken heart. They asked for Jesus to have mercy on Simon and to somehow use this to draw him to salvation. Finally, they prayed for God to help me forgive Simon so that bitterness wouldn't take root in my heart. The Holy Spirit spoke through my friends' intercession, reminding me that our pains here are not earthly battles. Ephesians 6:12 puts it clearly: "For our struggle is not against flesh and blood, but against the rulers, against the authorities, against the powers of this dark world and against the spiritual forces of evil in the heavenly realms." Though Simon's words had wounded me and poked at a sore spot in my heart, the real enemy was Satan. And his intention was to take me down and make me useless to the Lord's service.

Over the next few days, I prayed God would give me a forgiving spirit toward Simon. The pain of that man's words—and the insecurity they had ignited—washed over me again and again. I cried over them. A few days before I would return to California to find out if I would continue in the competition, the Lord led me to the book of Joshua during my personal quiet time.

In chapter 3, the Israelite leader is preparing to lead the people across the Jordan River and into the Promised Land. Joshua 3:5 stood out to me: "Joshua told the people, 'Consecrate yourselves, for tomorrow the LORD will do amazing things among you.'" God reminded me again that this journey wasn't about me, my flaws, or my insecurities. He had chosen me, and He wanted to speak through me. At that moment, I had no idea all that would entail, but a few days later, I would get my chance to represent Him to my biggest audience yet.

Getting Real

- Think of a time you felt out of place or intimidated. What made you feel this way?
- Name a time when God used you to speak His truth, encouragement, or comfort to someone else. What happened?
- God used my last event with Living Proof Live to prepare my heart for what I would experience during Hollywood week. Think of a time when God used something to prepare you for a season ahead. How did it come together for you?
- My friends ministered to me and comforted me in a moment when I was hurt and embarrassed. What are some of the benefits of doing life in community with others?
- Think of a time when God used someone else's words to encourage you or pull you out of a dark place. How can you do the same for someone else?

• five •

GOOD NEWS

I've been praying (how long?)
For so, so long
Believing (for what?)
That day would come
He heard me (yes, He did)
And He pulled me out
He put me right here for such a time as now

On January 23, I flew back to Hollywood for the semifinals. I had felt led to fast and pray for three days, leading up to seeing Simon again. My friends were praying for me—that I would be able to forgive him and that God would give me the words to say. The next time I saw Simon, I would also find out if I'd made it into the top twenty-four.

At the hotel, the contestants who'd made it through Hollywood week assembled in a large room. Ken and Nigel got onstage to explain what would happen next. One at a time, we would ride the elevator upstairs and walk the hallway to the judges' room. They encouraged us to not hold back our reactions about the premiere. Drama makes good television, and they wanted lots of it. Nigel looked directly at me and said, "If Simon was a jerk, tell him off! We want a reaction."

I had some things to say to Simon, all right. But I don't think they were what the producers were expecting.

THE MEANING OF FORGIVENESS

When Jesus was on earth, His disciple Peter once asked Him a provocative question. "Lord, how many times shall I forgive my brother or sister who sins against me? Up to seven times?"

I'm sure that seemed like a generous number to Peter. Scholars have suggested that he was asking how many times he should forgive the *same* person for the *same* offense. He was probably a bit taken aback by Jesus's answer.

"I tell you, not seven times, but seventy-seven times," Jesus said (Matthew 18:21–22).

Then He told a story about a master who was settling accounts with his servants. The first man who came before the master owed him ten thousand talents, which was the equivalent of millions of dollars in that time. The master ordered that everything the man owned, including his wife and children, be sold to repay the massive debt. But the servant begged for mercy, promising to repay all he owed.

The master took pity on him and forgave his entire debt. Just like that, the servant owed him nothing. Imagine the relief that man would have felt. He was about to have the worst day of his life but was handed the best day instead.

Right after the servant left the master's presence, he happened to run into a fellow servant who owed him one hundred denarii, which was equivalent to a few bucks. In a shocking display, the servant who had just been forgiven grabbed the man by the neck. "Pay back what you owe me!" he screamed.

The man fell to his knees, begging for mercy. "Be patient with me, and I will pay it back." He used the exact words the first man had spoken to the master.

But that first man refused to show mercy. He had his fellow servant thrown into prison until he could repay the money.

When the master found out about this event, he summoned the servant whose debt he had just forgiven. "You wicked servant," he said. "I canceled all that debt of yours because you begged me to. Shouldn't you have had mercy on your fellow servant just as I had on you?" Then he cast him into prison until he could repay all that he owed.

At the end of that story, Jesus delivered the mic drop: "This is how my heavenly Father will treat each of you unless you forgive your brother or sister from your heart" (Matthew 18:23–35).

I've come to realize that forgiveness isn't really about me or the person who hurt me. It's about accepting the mercy of the Father and paying it forward. It's about understanding the weight of the debt I owed before Jesus took my place. Because of Him, I can stand faultless before my Father in Heaven. I have been handed the best day ever—every single day.

THE GREEN MILE

As I sat on the bench, waiting to walk what we contestants jokingly called "the green mile"—the walk to the judges' room that could potentially be our last—Nigel once again came to me to ensure I knew what he was looking for. "You heard the comments Simon made about you, right?

When you get in there, we've instructed the judges to let you say whatever you want to say first. We can edit out anything that is not appropriate for family hour TV."

I raised an eyebrow. "Don't worry. I've got some choice words for Simon."

I thought of the speech I'd practiced inside my head dozens of times. Before my turn came, seven people went up, and seven came back down with sad faces and tears because they'd been cut. I couldn't believe it. Some of the strongest singers hadn't advanced. Ryan announced the next to walk "the mile" would be Katherine McPhee. With dark hair and eyes, Kat was not only stunningly beautiful; she also possessed a soulful, smooth-as-butter voice. So it was no surprise when she made the cut.

Ryan told me I was up. As I walked into the large room where the judges sat, the only sound was my boots clicking loudly on the hardwood floor. I sat down on a tiny chair opposite the judges' table and made a joke about how they didn't need a bigger stage but they could have gotten me a bigger chair. The judges laughed and seemed appreciative that I'd broken the ice. I took a deep breath and looked Simon square in the eye.

"Simon, a lot of people want me to say a lot of things to you," I began. "But this is what I want to say to you. Yes, you hurt me, and I cried. It was painful—it really was." I paused. Every eye in the room was focused on me. Every ear listened to hear what I would say next. Maybe they expected a barrage of expletives while wagging my finger and rolling my neck. I was certain they didn't expect what I said next. "I want you to know that I've forgiven you. And that you don't need someone to apologize in order to forgive them. I figured if Jesus could die so that all my wrongs could be forgiven, I can certainly extend that same grace to you. I just wanted you to know that."

As I said the words, I felt a weight lift from my heart.

"Amen!" Randy exclaimed.

Simon looked furtively from the producers behind me to my face and back again in shock. Then he spoke. "Mandisa, I'm humbled. Come here."

He stood from the table, walked over, and gave me a hug.

"I now feel one millimeter small," he said, returning to his seat, "so I suppose I'll carry on." He looked down at his notes before continuing. "I'm sorry to tell you," he began, "but . . . you are going to have to go through this again because you're through to the next round!"

I screamed and leaped up from my chair, thanking the judges. As I hugged Randy, he said, "I liked your speech. You said the right thing to us."

Then he turned to Simon. "Apologize, Simon."

As I spun around to leave the room, still dancing with excitement, I heard Simon utter words I never expected to hear: "I do apologize."

I walked out of that door feeling the freedom that comes from forgiveness. God had put me in that tiny hot seat to share His good news with Simon—and thirty million TV viewers. Through my friends' prayers and my small act of obedience, He had done amazing things.

SURVIVING THE SEMIFINALS

After heading back to Nashville for two weeks, I returned to Hollywood on February 20 for the semifinal round. We had been told to be prepared to stay until May 25, which was the end of the competition. During the following three weeks, there would be three live shows per week, with two men and two women being eliminated each week. The pace was grueling, but I continued to turn in performances I felt good about. In between my Chicago audition and the semifinals, I had lost thirty pounds from working out and eating a healthy diet, so I also came into this round of competition feeling more confident.

When I wasn't practicing or performing, I spent a lot of time praying and journaling. I was still seeking the Lord's plan for me being on the show. During those weeks, He gave me many opportunities to interact with people who were different from me (and even a few who required extra grace, if you know what I mean). We had spiritual conversations, and a few of us even attended church together.

Each week, as I prayed for my fellow contestants, my prayers would be drawn to a certain person. Recording my specific prayers for that contestant in my journal and then seeing that person eliminated made me feel like God was letting me in on things to come. I also felt as though God revealed to me that I would make it into the top three. Of course, I *wanted* to make it to the end of the competition, but this impression was more than my own desires. I felt it so strongly, I wrote the words in my journal. I had no reason not to believe what I'd heard. After all, God had revealed many similar details to me through this journey that had already happened.

Week three of the semifinals, I wowed the judges and audience with my rendition of Chaka Khan's "I'm Every Woman." After my performance, Randy said, "This is the best vocal by a female this season. She just set the benchmark, girls. This is the one to beat!"

"I got chills," Paula said.

Then it was Simon's turn. "Mandisa, every one of these girls is going to hate your guts tonight. Because you made everyone who appeared before you appear ordinary. It was in a completely and utterly different league."

I was flattered and felt it was confirmation for the words I'd written in my journal. I made it through to the top twelve, and magazines and entertainment news began to predict that I might be the last woman standing—up against Taylor Hicks or Chris Daughtry. It was exciting to hear predictions that I might be in that coveted top three, or even a contender for first place!

Each week of the finals had a theme. The first week we sang songs by Stevie Wonder. When I sang for the legendary artist, he said, "She could sing anything!" That week I turned in an energetic performance of "Don't You Worry 'Bout a Thing."

The next week featured tunes from the 1950s, and I had the privilege of being coached by Barry Manilow, who told me to call him up if nothing came of *Idol*. I sang Dinah Washington's version of "I Don't Hurt Anymore," which was one of my favorite performances of the competition.

With those two showings, I arrived at the top ten. This was a big deal because whatever happened, the top ten would reunite for an *American Idol* tour in the summer. Crossing this milestone also felt spiritually significant. I increasingly felt the nudge to be bold in my faith.

My thoughts turned to Esther, the young Jewish woman who became queen of Persia and saved her people from destruction. At one point, her cousin Mordecai said to her, "And who knows but that you have come to your royal position for such a time as this?" (Esther 4:14). Because Esther was obedient to her unusual calling—winning a contest and becoming queen and influencing the king—God used her to save the Jews. I wondered if I was on *American Idol* for such a time as this. I wanted to be intentional—not only in how I lived my life and interacted with others, but also in what I proclaimed from the stage.

The first week as top-ten contenders, we were asked to sing songs from the 2000s. Producers explained that this was the week to show the judges and the world the kind of artists we wanted to be after the season ended. I chose one of my favorite songs of all time: Mary Mary's "Shackles (Praise You)." The song, which proclaims freedom in Christ, was deeply personal to me as I sought liberation from many of the things I felt bound by, including childhood wounds, food addiction, and insecurity about my body. I hoped my proclamation would also encourage those listening to see that freedom was available to anyone. Before my performance, I emailed my intercessors, asking them to pray for me, the judges, and the audience.

I asked them to join me in praying we would all experience God in a new way.

I had planned to wear a red football jersey with the words *Galatians 5:1* on the front. The verse says, "It is for freedom that Christ has set us free. Stand firm, then, and do not let yourselves be burdened again by a yoke of slavery." After dress rehearsal, and moments before I took the stage for the live show, I was told I wouldn't be allowed to wear the shirt. This news frazzled me, and I searched for something new to wear, but I knew the show must go on. Emboldened by the last-minute distraction, and sensing the prayers being lifted for me, I clapped my hands to the beat as I walked onstage. "This song goes out to everybody who wants to be free!" I said. "Your addiction, lifestyle, and situation may be big, but God is bigger." I sang the song with all my heart, as I had so many times before on the Living Proof Live worship team. As I let my voice ring out, I thought about the shackles God had released in my own life, and I truly praised Him. When the song ended, the audience went wild. They stood and clapped their hands. I lifted my own hands in applause to the Lord.

The judges, however, were less enthusiastic. Randy didn't dig it and nodded his head in disappointment. Paula told me she'd like me to sing something *more* vulnerable. (If only she knew!) And Simon called my song choice "indulgent" and said he just didn't get it. That was a moment when I understood that obedience doesn't always feel good. Yes, sometimes doing the right thing leads to accolades from others, but that's not always the case. In fact, sometimes the things most precious to God are misunderstood, dismissed, and even ridiculed by the world. In 1 Corinthians 2:14, it puts it this way, "But people who aren't spiritual can't receive these truths from God's Spirit. It all sounds foolish to them and they can't understand it, for only those who are spiritual can understand what the Spirit means" (NLT). Totally separate from how awesome or poorly I sang that night, much of the world wouldn't "get it" when it came to the truths that song told about God.

Thankfully, due to the votes of those who *did* get it, I made it through to the next week—country week. I figured the country-style singers Kellie Pickler and Bucky Covington had a natural advantage, but after a decade of living in Nashville, I hoped to make my city proud. I chose Shania Twain's "Any Man of Mine" because it was fun and upbeat, and I knew I could work the crowd. But when my performance ended, once again, the judges' responses were less than enthusiastic. Randy called it a "weird song choice," and Simon said the song was "horrible." I went home that night feeling that I'd turned in a second-rate performance and let down Music City.

The following night the nine of us stood onstage, waiting to find out who was going home. I hoped my performance had been good enough to get me through to the next round. We stood in three groups—one of which was the bottom three. Because I was with Elliott Yamin and Paris Bennett, and none of us had been in the bottom three yet, I felt pretty good about our chances. But when the other two groups of three were declared safe, my stomach lurched. Finally, only Elliott and I remained on the stage with Ryan. That's when he said the words I'd been dreading. I had been eliminated.

The crowd gasped, and my fellow contestants looked stunned. I was as shocked as they were. I kept thinking about the words I'd written in my journal. *I was supposed to make it into the top three.* After I left the stage, I was immediately escorted into a room to talk to a counselor. (You would be surprised how emotionally devastating getting cut can be.) I had talked with this counselor before. During this interview, he told me he wasn't concerned about me. He knew I had support at home and a foundation of faith. In a moment of total honesty, I blurted, "Yes, but right now I'm feeling shaky because I feel like the Lord told me something that didn't come to pass. I don't know if He changed His mind or if I heard Him wrong."

That thought continued to plague me as I went through a week of talk show appearances and radio interviews. As it turned out, everyone wanted to talk to me about my five-second intro to "Shackles," where I had said, "Your addiction, lifestyle, and situation may be big, but God is bigger." When I said those words, I was thinking about my own lifestyle of overeating and food addiction. I figured there were people watching who might have similar struggles. However, the word *lifestyle* had sparked a controversy, as some people assumed I was being antigay. I found myself on the defensive, trying to explain my beliefs with grace and truth, only to be met with attack. It felt like the world had turned against me, and the firestorm magnified my feelings of disappointment about being eliminated. I began to wonder if I'd done any good at all.

Even though it was painful at the time, I now see that those questions gave me an opportunity to share the good news of the gospel over and over. I told people I was a Christian. I told them I had believed in Jesus and His work on the cross for salvation and forgiveness for my sin. I told them I believed the Bible was the accurate Word of God and that I tried to live my life according to its principles. I explained that I wasn't perfect but that being in a relationship with Jesus is what makes me a Christian. I told them that anyone who trusts in Jesus by faith can be saved and have eternal life.

After a week of interviews and media engagements, I was allowed to go home. I arrived home feeling defeated and discouraged. I described my depression in my 2007 book *Idoleyes*:

> I turned and snuggled in my pillow, not wanting to hear from God. I thought I had been depending on the Lord. I had begged Him to open up the windows of heaven and pour out blessings on everyone who roomed with me or heard me sing from the time I reached Hollywood until the time I hit the top three—or had that been *my* plan?
>
> No answers came. I languished in my pitiful weakness and didn't leave the apartment for several days. I sheltered myself for a long time— ordered a lot of pizza, slept too much, and didn't bathe. Didn't unpack, either; I only slept, ate, and watched TV.
>
> When the phone rang, I ignored it and let the answering machine take a message. Soon I began

to hear people saying, "We just want to know if you're alive."[1]

Looking back, I can see how depression—and the resulting isolation, overeating, and shame—has been a pattern in my life. Even when I was a child, food was always the thing I turned to when I was sad. When my dad and stepmom moved to Texas, I found solace in ice cream and chips. When I was raped as a teenager and my guilt and shame threatened to crush me, my way of coping had been to retreat and eat. I had carried those negative patterns with me through my teen years and into my adult life.

After I was cut from *American Idol*, I felt like a failure and was angry at God. I felt like He had misled me. I'd been walking with Him every step of the way. I had chosen obedience, and now I wondered if He had abandoned me. Instead of taking my disappointment and confusion to the Father, I turned to food. Instead of eating a couple of donuts, I would eat a dozen. After a few days of questioning whether I could hear God's voice, I stopped trying to talk to Him. The chasm between us felt wide and dark.

A month later I returned to Hollywood to be part of the finale. The final showdown was between Taylor

Hicks—who ended up winning that season—and Katherine McPhee. That night, the top six female contestants performed a medley. At the end of the song, I reprised my "I'm Every Woman" performance. I closed out the song with a high note that brought down the house. The crowd leaped to its feet in wild applause. I heard Ryan announce they'd just added fifteen new concert dates to the *American Idol* tour, which would take place that summer. My time on the stage wasn't finished. Not even close.

I'm thankful I was part of season five of *American Idol* (which happened to be the most highly rated season of the show). Many in the top ten went on to have successful careers in music, Broadway, and even TV and movies. Being on *American Idol* was a roller coaster of an experience, a ride that's given me some of my highest highs and lowest lows.

The night I was eliminated, I had one last dinner with my fellow contestants. Over pasta, chicken parmesan, and garlic bread, these people, now dear friends, took turns toasting (and roasting) me. Taylor stood and smiled. "Now that you're gone, Mandisa, we're all going to hell," he said. The others laughed at his joke. Then, in a serious tone, he told me it meant a lot to know I was praying for them. I nodded. Ace commented on my pure heart. Paris said I was like a big sister to her. And through a shower of tears, Kellie told me I was one of the godliest women she had ever known, and that she looked up to me.

I was touched by their words and reminded that they saw me not only as a fellow contestant but also as a person who was walking out her Christian faith. That was exactly what I had asked the Lord to let me be.

When I finally stood to say my goodbyes to a room of people with whom I shared such a special bond, I was so full of emotion I could barely speak. I told my friends how much their words had meant to me. I told them I expected great things from them, and that I would be praying for them. I told them what an honor it had been to be part of *their* season—the best season—of *American Idol.*

Getting Real

- Do you find it easy or difficult to forgive?
- How does the story of the unforgiving debtor in Matthew 18 cause you to look at forgiveness in a new light?
- Is there someone in your life you need to forgive?

- Have you ever taken a bold stand for Christ and experienced a backlash for it? How did God use that situation for His glory?
- Think of a time when you felt that God let you down. How did you respond? What did you learn about who God is? About yourself?

six

THE DEFINITION
OF ME

I want the love, I want the light
I want the beauty on the inside
I want the One that you can't see to be the definition of me

More than the face, more than the girl
More than the voice, more than the world
I want the truth that I believe to be the definition of me

After my time on *American Idol* and a successful summer tour, life began to pick up for me. I met with many different labels—mainstream R&B labels, gospel labels, and all the main contemporary Christian music labels. In 2007, I signed my first record deal with EMI/Sparrow (now Capitol Records). I released my first CCM album, *True Beauty*, later that year. The title song, "True

Beauty," is the first song I wrote—while the pain was still fresh from Simon's comments about my weight. Most of the messages in the songs I write come from my own experiences and the lessons God is teaching me through them. Exploring where true beauty is found has always been, and I imagine always will be, one of those lessons.

Through the title song of that first album, I declared that my outward appearance, including my size, doesn't dictate my value. God cares more about what's on the inside because He intricately designed *all* of who I am. That's easy to say (and sing); it's harder to believe. When it comes to my feelings on beauty, let's just say . . . it's complicated. I like to look good. Who doesn't? One of my strongest love languages is "words of affirmation." So when someone compliments me on my appearance, I feel valued and loved. But when I was sixteen and my rapist kept telling me how beautiful I was, I think I subconsciously associated outward beauty with danger. My experience taught me that being pretty was a liability that threatened my safety. Ever since then, I've struggled with feeling like there's something wrong with outward beauty or wanting to look beautiful. In my attempt to protect myself, I could be dismissive of physical beauty (and claim it wasn't for me) because, hey, the Bible says God cares more about what's on the inside anyway.

There was a time when I equated beauty with vanity and superficiality, but I've come to realize that God has designed beautiful things. Sunsets. Oceans. Flowers. Faces. So many things in this world are truly amazing to look at. God created us to enjoy beautiful things and people, and beauty has a purpose. Going back to the story of Esther in the Bible, her beauty played a vital role in God's plan to save the Jews. Had she not been beautiful, she would not have been chosen to be the queen of Persia. Because of her royal position, she was able to save her people.

I have come to understand that God is the great Designer—of both inward and outward beauty. In 1 Samuel 16:7, God tells Samuel, "The LORD does not look at the things people look at. People look at the outward appearance, but the LORD looks at the heart." I used to read those words and think they meant that physical beauty didn't matter. But that same chapter points out more than once that David was indeed a hottie (verses 12 and 18). As a matter of fact, when King Saul was being troubled by a tormenting spirit, being easy on the eyes actually helped David land a coveted position playing music for him. But David was more than outwardly appealing. That God called him a "man after his own heart" suggests that David had a beauty of mind, spirit, and character that God delighted in (1 Samuel 13:14).

As I've grown in my relationship with God, I've realized that beauty is good because it is created by God. Still, that unfading, true beauty that 1 Peter 3:3–4 talks about shines from the inside out, and that is the kind most precious to God. Regardless of how we look, we can have a radiance that comes from the Lord. Psalm 34:5 says, "Those who look to him are radiant; their faces are never covered with shame." As someone who battles with shame, especially about my body, that verse has always meant a lot to me.

DEFINING SUCCESS

As much as I wanted to make music that was authentic and encouraging, I also wanted my record label to be happy with its sales. My *True Beauty* album turned in a solid performance, selling 17,000 copies the first week (and debuting at number 43 on the US Billboard 200 chart). My label was pleased and felt the album did well, but a former reality TV show contestant in the Christian music industry was an unproven commodity. My numbers were nothing compared to the record sales of some of my fellow *Idol* contestants. Winner Taylor Hicks's album debuted at the number 2 spot on the Billboard 200 chart and sold 298,000 copies its first week! Chris Daughtry's debut album became the fastest-selling debut rock album in history, selling more than a million copies in five weeks. Katherine McPhee's album also debuted at number 2 on the Billboard 200, selling 116,000 copies in its first week. Even Bucky Covington's album sold 61,000 copies on week one. As I compared myself to the incredible successes of my fellow finalists, I felt like a loser. Looking back, my album did amazingly well by CCM standards of the time. It debuted number 1 on the Christian albums chart, but I was so caught up in the "comparison trap" that I couldn't recognize my own success.

My first radio single, "Only the World"—an upbeat, pop, R&B tune—released to radio in spring 2007. I hoped the radio stations would play it, but I recognized that my sound was a bit different from what I would normally hear on CCM stations. What if I wasn't accepted? Would my label drop me? What would I do then? You can imagine my relief and elation the first time I heard the song blaring through my car speakers as I drove down a curvy Tennessee road. If you happened to be near Nashville in May 2007 and saw a Black woman pulling over a red Toyota, freaking out, and pointing her phone at her stereo, that was probably me. To this day, whenever I hear one of my songs playing on one of my local stations, I typically squeal with glee and pump up the volume as loud as I can stand. I never want to take that for granted. "Only the World" did great on the Christian radio charts, rising to number 6 among CCM singles of the time. Over the next few months, my label released two more slower and reflective singles from my album: "God Speaking" and "Voice of a Savior." They did not climb the charts as much as my first single, and I quickly realized I would need to decide how to define success in my life and career. If I compared myself to other artists, I could always find people who were much more successful. People always packed larger stadiums and sold more albums. But I began to notice that some of my songs that didn't climb the charts were the ones God seemed to use the most.

Although the song "God Speaking" didn't do as well on the radio, when I sang it in concert, I could see the impact it had on people. The messages I received expressed how the comforting and encouraging lyrics resonated with listeners as they sought God's direction. That is when I began to learn that I would drive myself crazy if I allowed chart position to be the main barometer of success. The highs would feel great, but the lows would not. I would need to set my mind on things above and pray that God would somehow use my offerings for His glory. As I asked the Holy Spirit to help me see my career

THE DEFINITION OF ME

through His eyes, He began to reshape my views of what determined success.

When *True Beauty* was released, I was still an unknown entity, and the industry was still trying to figure out how this "Mandisa thing" was gonna work. I soon learned that in music, just like in any entertainment industry, you can be typecast. I found myself as the "upbeat, R&B, power anthem girl," while it seemed the radio industry looked to other artists, such as my girl Natalie Grant, to provide the more melodic spiritual ballads.

In 2009, I released my second album, *Freedom*. My label and I discovered a groove and began to figure out what Christian radio wanted from me: upbeat, get-up-and-dance, encouraging anthems. The single "My Deliverer" quickly rose to the top ten on the charts. My next album, *What If We Were Real* (2011), brought me my first number 1 hit: "Stronger."

GETTING STRONGER

I felt like a baby deer learning to walk during those first formative years as an artist. Being faced with sudden fame while balancing healthy relationships, taking care of myself physically, and making smart business decisions forced me to become stronger emotionally, spiritually, and physically.

After *American Idol*, churches and organizations started requesting me to come do full concerts. I needed a band! I had always been part of someone else's band but had never put one together myself. Thankfully, my manager, Dan Pitts, set me up with a bass player he thought would make a great musical director. A musical director puts together players and rehearses the music to create the sound. The moment I met Bernard Harris, I knew he and I would work well together. I trusted his input on a keyboard player, guitarist, and drummer to travel on the road for concerts. It was important to me that the players were not just quality musicians, but also people who genuinely loved Jesus and sought to serve Him both onstage and off.

While I left the instrumentalists to Bernard, I already had in mind whom I wanted to sing background vocals with me on the road. Kisha Mitchell was the first person I called. From the years of her leading me in praise at Greater Grace, I knew her powerful voice and heart for worship would be a perfect fit. Because of this new world of moving from the back of the stage to the front, having a friend with me on the road would give me a sense of comfort I could not have felt otherwise. She started traveling on the road with me in 2007.

THE DEFINITION OF ME

I also asked my friend Myshel Wilkins, whom I had met in college and become friends with when we both worked at Lifeway. Eventually I met Laura Cooksey, who later became one of my best friends as we traveled together. Laura, Kisha, Myshel, and I called ourselves the OGs ("Original Gangsters") and became incredibly close on the road. When you spend most of your waking hours with the same people, it's impossible to not become really close.

Whenever the OGs and I reminisce about those early days, a concert we gave near my hometown of Sacramento always comes to mind. Laughing about the fiasco that unfolded that night never fails to leave our stomachs sore. It was the first time we performed "The Definition of Me." Knowing the song would be unfamiliar to my audience because it was from my recent album, and not a radio single, I placed it in the middle of the set after some of the recognizable, high-energy songs. I didn't want the message of the song to get lost in the funky beat, so I spent a few moments talking about my recent struggles with finding my identity in Jesus rather than the number on the bathroom scale or the reflection in the mirror. Whenever we're performing a song for the first time, the band has this crazy nervous energy. The musicians want to make sure the band hits are synced, and every intro and outro goes off without a hitch. And the singers want to sing the right lyrics in the right spots with every note in tune.

That night, Myshel had the added pressure of rapping for the first time. I had charged her with the rap portion of the song—called "spittin' bars"—originally performed by Blanca Callahan (from Group 1 Crew, one of my favorite artists). Myshel had practiced incessantly, but the wordiness proved overwhelming. She wrote the words on her hand, hoping they would jog her memory if needed. I ended my sharing time with the proclamation, "I will no longer bow to what the world says I should be. I choose to let Jesus be the definition of me!"

I pointed to Bernard, his cue to start the music. But no music; just awkward silence. My pulse quickened as I turned around to look at my music director and saw Myshel staring at her hand for a last-minute study session. But I saw no trace of Kisha!

While the audience stirred, Laura mouthed to me, "She had to go to the bathroom." Maybe the bathroom emergency was caused by the anxiety of debuting a new song. More likely, it was more about Kisha's attention to hydration during the long flight from Tennessee to California. Whatever the cause, I knew the show must go on. I've never been great at stopping the six-inch journey a thought takes from my mind to my mouth. After bluntly explaining that my soprano had to "use it," I told the band to start without her. By the time we rounded into the second chorus, and right before Myshel's rap premiere, I saw Kisha out of the corner of my eye and motioned her up onstage. The roaring applause from the audience as she made her triumphant return provided a moment of levity before Myshel joined me front of stage for her rap debut. She will never live down what happened next. In her defense, at least she got the first line right—the next seven, not so much. It came out sounding something like this:

They say I'm cute with the boots and the trendy attire
A sumanama shamaybooya keeko sodumakiya
But eenie meenie miney mama
God's-a-comin in a Honda . . .

Needless to say, I waited a few years before attempting that song in concert again! But the laughter that occurred, both onstage and in our gracious audience, is a memory I will cherish forever. My band became like family. After a woman in the audience told Bernard that the music we did onstage was like "glorious funk," I dubbed the band with that very name. Glorious Funk and I traveled from California to Maine to everywhere in between. And those were some of the best days of my life.

SEEKING FREEDOM

During summer 2009, I performed at a festival in South Dakota, and the band and I had a chance to check out Mount Rushmore during the day. That experience opened my eyes to the reality of my physical condition. My friends and fellow musicians easily made the trek from the entrance of the national memorial to the lookout area, but I found myself huffing and puffing with constant back pain. That evening, during our one-hour set, I was painfully aware of how out of shape I was. I struggled to get through the singing, dancing, and speaking. After the performance, in a moment of vulnerability, I told Kisha, Myshel, and Laura that I had to do something. In all of my talk about true beauty and not being defined by society's standards of beauty and worth, I had gone too far in the opposite direction. I wasn't treating my body like the temple of the Holy Spirit that it was (1 Corinthians 6:19). I was doing what was permissible, but not what was beneficial; I was allowing food to be my master. And I was the heaviest I had been up to that point.

I asked my friends to keep me accountable on the road and to check in on me at home. There is something about having friends who just "get you"—people who accept you just as you are but are also quick to see your potential and push you toward it. Proverbs 18:24 says, "One who has unreliable friends soon comes to ruin, but there is a friend who sticks closer than a brother." Kisha, Myshel, and Laura were those kinds of friends to me.

I decided to hire a trainer and get healthy. I knew breaking free from food addiction wouldn't be easy. For most of my life, I had turned to food and emotional eating, but I knew that God wanted me to be a healthy, whole person He could fully use. The extra weight affected my confidence, how I could move onstage, and my endurance during concerts. I knew Jesus was the only One who could set me free from this lifelong struggle.

The Bible has a lot to say about freedom. Here are a few of my favorite verses on the topic:

"So if the Son sets you free, you will be free indeed." (John 8:36)

"You, my brothers and sisters, were called to be free. But do not use your freedom to indulge the flesh; rather, serve one another humbly in love." (Galatians 5:13)

"Now the Lord is the Spirit, and where the Spirit of the Lord is, there is freedom." (2 Corinthians 3:17)

Freedom is something God wants for us, y'all. We get so bogged down with our sin, our addictions, and our habits. These things are like shackles, keeping us from the life of freedom God desires for us. But Jesus came to make us free! I knew that God wanted me to be free from my food addiction and the shame I felt. To lose the weight, I didn't go on a diet . . . exactly. While restrictive diets have always caused me to lose weight quickly, I found that the moment I ate a biscuit, I would immediately put the pounds back on, plus some. Whatever I did to take off the weight, I knew I would have to continue doing to keep it off. I needed to change my mindset, not just my habits and behaviors. As I ate a diet focused on fruits, vegetables, lean protein, and healthy fiber, I made my mealtimes a conversation with God. When I was tempted—that "Hot Now" sign at Krispy Kreme was serious warfare—I would turn scriptures such as 1 Corinthians 10:13 into a prayer: "Father, I know that no temptation exists except what is common to man. Your Word says that You will not allow me to be tempted beyond what I can bear. I confess that I am tempted by the thought of a hot glazed donut melting in my mouth right now. I am asking You to provide a way out, so I can stand up under this temptation." More often than not, audibly expressing my need to the Lord gave me the strength to resist. The more I practiced this, the stronger I got, and the closer I felt to my Savior.

I also grew stronger physically. Along with working out with my personal trainer, Tina, I discovered Zumba, a type of fitness dancing that uses Latin and hip-hop music. For the first time in my life, exercise felt fun. I called my quest to lose one hundred pounds "Journey to 100" and made my progress public through videos on my website. Putting myself out there was embarrassing and uncomfortable, but I knew there were others going through similar struggles. In one video I said, "This is for any of you who are struggling with an area where you feel bound— any of you who may have something you thought you would never be free from. I really hope as I go through this journey, you can come along with me and we can do it together with the help of God."

Another video revealed a typical session with Trainer Tina, which involved about forty minutes a day of cardio, circuit training, and intervals. I said, "I know there are a lot of you that struggle in this area like I do. I want you to know you are not alone. This is the most difficult thing I have been through in my life, but it is so worth it in the end if it helps someone else overcome the way God is helping me overcome. Through God, all things are possible."

I received some amazing messages of encouragement from the people following along with my journey. They expressed how my honesty had given them hope and inspired them to take steps toward freedom in their own lives. 2 Corinthians 1:4 says that God "comforts us in all our troubles, so that we can comfort those in any trouble with the comfort we ourselves receive from God." I strongly believe this. In the process of changing my mindset and habits, God was comforting me, and I knew He had called me to offer others hope too.

After making a lot of progress and losing seventy-five pounds, I hit a plateau. Nothing I was doing seemed to be helping me lose the additional pounds. I was so discouraged. And what do I do when I'm discouraged? I eat a cookie (or five). Over the summer I slipped back into some of my old habits. I still worked out, but I ate whatever (and whenever) I wanted and gained back several pounds.

Spoiler alert: Turning to food when difficult emotions hit has continued to be a struggle for me. In fact, emotional eating may be something like the "thorn in the flesh" Paul describes in 2 Corinthians 12:7, and something I always struggle with. The upside of this struggle is that through it, I understand that God's grace is sufficient and His power is made perfect in my weakness. This thorn, and my awareness of my weakness, keeps me clinging to Him and His amazing grace. As I said in one of my "Journey to 100" videos, "Sometimes I fail, but God's mercies are new every morning. When you fall, get right back up and start again." Getting healthy is less about the destination, and more about the journey and what God teaches us along the way.

With my dependence on the Holy Spirit, the help of my community, and good old-fashioned hard work, I persevered. On February 15, 2011, the first single, "Stronger," from my upcoming album, debuted. How appropriate that on that day, when I stepped on the scale, I looked down and saw that I had officially lost one hundred pounds! Had my neighbors been home, I'm certain the sounds of my screams and the pounding of me jumping up and down would have been alarming. The "Journey to 100" was incredible, but the destination was pretty exciting too! On my final video, I said, "When we walk things out with God, as difficult as they are, He's able to bring us out stronger than we were before." I shared with those following my journey the five things I felt had led to my success:

- I relied on the Word of God, the most powerful tool we have in any battle as believers. Memorizing and reciting scripture helped me stay strong and resist temptation. There is an otherworldly power in the Word of God.
- I ate more whole grains, fruits, and vegetables, and I limited foods that I knew were not the healthiest choices for me.
- I exercised. It felt great to get my body moving. The accountability of having a trainer, plus my newfound love of Zumba and workout buddies, kept me motivated. Eventually, exercise became something I actually enjoyed.
- I saw a therapist who specialized in eating disorders, and she helped me identify some of the roots of why I turn to food.
- I prayed . . . a lot. In moments of temptation, God was right there.

Looking back, there is no way I could have achieved my goal without my supportive community. It was my friend Lasonya who invited me to my first Zumba class, and we danced our hearts out together two or three times a week. Laura, Lasonya, and I got together every so often for something we called "Fat Nights" (later changing its title to "Fit Nights" to keep it positive). We shot cooking videos of us transforming recipes we loved into healthier versions. Many of my friends, including Kisha, prayed for me, encouraged me, and listened when I was going through a hard time or felt like I'd hit a wall.

As human beings, we are *made* to have others in our lives to bolster us when we face challenges or hardships. We also need others to celebrate our victories. Scripture tells us: "Rejoice with those who rejoice; mourn with those who mourn" (Romans 12:15). We need each other; we are better together. I so easily forget this and think I have to do things on my own—that I have to hide myself when I mess up and "fix" myself before venturing back out into community. But my weight loss journey of two-plus years showed me how valuable those relationships are and how they help us experience the freedom God offers.

At my "100 Pound Party" I felt like I was on top of the world. On some level, I felt like I'd cracked the code for walking in freedom and victory—that I finally had life figured out. As my friends gathered around me, rejoicing with me in my success, life was good. I recently heard someone say that life is a paradox—with good and hard happening in our lives at all times. Sometimes the good outweighs the hard, and sometimes the hard outweighs the good—but they coexist.

As Ecclesiastes says, "There is a time for everything, and a season for every activity under the heavens: a time to be born and a time to die, a time to plant and a time to uproot, a time to kill and a time to heal, a time to tear down and a time to build, a time to weep and a time to laugh, a time to mourn and a time to dance" (3:1–4).

Joy and sorrow, life and death, gain and loss—all of these things are inextricably linked in this life. After I met my weight loss goal, I had two of the best years of my life. I was energized onstage, I felt connected with my family and friends, and my relationship with God soared to new heights. It felt like I was finally living the abundant life God had for me, free from some of my past sins and struggles. I was on a new path, and I was excited. But I suppose the saying "All good things must come to an end" has some truth to it. The thing is, when it was time to come down from the mountaintop, I was not prepared for what awaited me in the valley.

Getting Real

- Talk about a time when you fell into the comparison trap and were tempted to base your value on your performance.

- On tour, I became close with Kisha, Laura, and Myshel. Think of a close friend you've had in the past or currently have. How does that person encourage you? How do you encourage them?

- How do you define success? How do you think God defines success? (Look up Micah 6:8, Galatians 5:22–23, and Colossians 3:23–24 for ideas.)

- God offers us freedom through His Son. What are some ways God manifests that freedom in our lives? (Examples could include forgiving our sin, offering us new mercies, strengthening us to walk on the right path, giving us community, protecting us from the enemy's attacks, etc.)

- My community was vital in me achieving my weight loss goal. How have your friends helped you reach a goal or navigate a difficult season?

- In life, good and hard coexist. Talk about one good thing in your life right now and one hard thing. How is God present and at work in each?

seven

IT'S NOT OVER

You're right here in the questions
In the quiet You're still speaking
You're out here in the unknown
In the lowest low You're still reaching

Nothing lost and nothing wasted
I'm steady in Your hand
Even now You're orchestrating a miracle
It's not over

The words of "It's Not Over" felt so timely when I released the single in 2020. That was an un-paralleled year filled with questions about the future, God's presence, and His purposes. But my friends Rita Springer and Cavanaugh James actually wrote the cho-rus of that song in 2014. These are the words they put to music that summer: "It's not over. Something good is coming. It's not over. You'll finish what you started." If I had heard those words that summer, I'm not sure I would have believed them. Even though I'd been a Christian for over twenty years, the enemy was waging war on my heart and mind in an unprecedented way.

The day I got the text from Breonus telling me Kisha had died, I was in shock. Her sweet baby boy, Brennon, was just a year old. Even though I knew Kisha's health had been failing, I had fully believed God would heal her. When He didn't do that—at least in the way I was expecting—I felt betrayed, angry, disappointed. I didn't understand how a God who was just and good could allow such bad things to happen to those He loved. Didn't He know how it would devastate everyone who loved Kisha? He had to know how grief would threaten to swallow and even destroy me. The difficult truth was, He did know—and yet He still allowed it. And because of that, I wasn't sure I could trust Him.

Everything in me wanted to run and hide—just like that little California girl who ran to her bedroom with a box of sugary cereal after overhearing a classmate's cruel words. Or like the young woman who stayed home for a month and ordered enough pizza to feed an army after being eliminated from a singing competition. I longed to get away from people and comfort myself the best way I knew how—with food.

But I had obligations to fulfill. I wasn't even halfway through the summer festival season, and I had already committed to TobyMac's Hits Deep Tour that fall. Running away wasn't an option, at least not right away. So I kept going, but it got harder and harder to believe what I was singing. While my mouth sang about being freed from captivity, my mind would turn to the cancer that had held Kisha captive. It didn't *feel* like God had delivered her. As my voice rang out, "He is with you when your faith is dead, and you can't even get out of bed," I longed to *be* in bed nursing my dying faith.

The high point of every concert that summer was the song "Overcomer," which had become my most successful song and album to date. It skyrocketed to number 1 on the radio charts and sold more albums than my previous three recordings. Each of my previous albums had been nominated, but *Overcomer* won the Grammy Award for Best Contemporary Christian Music Album. I should have been elated. But every time I sang, "You're an overcomer" and implored the audience to "stay in the fight 'til the final round," I couldn't help but think of when Kisha's final round had ended: June 29, 2014. While I sang hope over those facing their own battles, my hope was hitting rock bottom.

It was a slow fade into the darkness. For a while, I pushed the doubts swirling in my head to the side as I celebrated God onstage. Those times on the road felt like the light of day. But once the tour bus pulled back into Nashville, my time at home was the darkness of night— binge-eating, sleeping, and isolating myself from everyone. Then another round of performances would come, and I'd find myself in a cycle of darkness to light and back again.

At the time of Kisha's diagnosis in 2013, I was the healthiest I'd been in years. I was strong and energetic, and my stage presence blossomed. I added dancers to Glorious Funk, so our concerts were filled with high-energy movement and worship. I even added some of my own Latin-style choreography (inspired by Zumba) to my performances and dubbed it "Mandisercise." My "Good Morning" dance routine was on YouTube, so when we performed the choreography onstage during the crowd-pleasing hit, it was always a highlight to see the crowd joining in.

I loved that my weight loss journey had been an inspiration to others, but in the months following Kisha's death, I rapidly put the weight back on. I felt unmotivated and stopped training with Tina and quit attending my Zumba class. Soon my onstage dancing was my only exercise. Without relying on the Comforter to provide a way out of temptation, I regularly gave in to the neon-light allure of the "Hot Now" Krispy Kreme sign. Instead of feeding on the Bread of Life, I stuffed myself with regular old bread—cheese biscuits from Red Lobster and Mama's Pancake Breakfast from Cracker Barrel. Any carb would do. As I abandoned the lifestyle that had allowed me to shed the pounds, my body quickly returned to its prior shape.

I was miserable—physically, emotionally, and spiritually. Rather than dancing around the stage, I would pull a stool to the middle of the stage and sit. My dancers did their high-energy routine while I sat there, trying to catch enough breath to sing. Some of my fans wrote to me, asking if I was okay and saying I didn't seem like myself. I *wasn't* myself! I couldn't even stand up for ten minutes without my back aching.

My physical pain only added to the deep emotional pain I was feeling. "Overcomer" was a bona fide hit, but it was also the hardest song for me to sing. I felt this dichotomy. The inspirational anthem was the highlight of my performance, but when I sang it, all I wanted was to get off the stage and eat.

I began passing on the tour requests rolling in. After a demanding schedule had kept me so busy, I told my manager that I needed a break. Not working gave me even more time to myself. I stopped going to church and isolated myself in my house. I neglected my daily devotional times, didn't crack open my Bible, and pushed away everything that had to do with Jesus. Rather than starting my day in prayer and the Word, I would start my day by turning on the TV and lying in bed, filling my mind with the imaginary lives of the characters on my screen. My only movement was from my bed upstairs, down sixteen steps to my recliner downstairs, and back again. By the time I hit rock bottom in 2016, I peaked at close to four hundred pounds. I felt hopeless, ashamed, and lonely.

While I know the introvert in me needed some time by myself following the loss of Kisha and a chaotic, busy touring season, there's a thin line between healthy alone time and isolation. First Peter 5:8 warns: "Be alert and of sober mind. Your enemy the devil prowls around like a roaring lion looking for someone to devour." The devil has sinister plans, and he's really, really good at what he does. His objective is to take us down and diminish the glory of God shining out of us.

In my pain and confusion, I let down my guard, and Satan cunningly took advantage of the opportunity to try to devour me. Alone in my house day after day, I abused my spirit and mistreated my body. Dark and destructive musings started overtaking my mind. The scary thing about those thoughts is that they made a lot of sense. *You could feel relief right now. You could be there with Kisha and Jesus and the pain would be gone. You're saved; God will forgive you.*

John 8:44 says that when Satan lies, "he speaks his native language, for he is a liar and the father of lies." I've fallen victim to those lies so many times throughout my life. The thing I've noticed is that he's sneaky about it. He often takes a little truth and twists it for his own purposes. The book of Matthew talks about the time where Jesus was led by the Spirit into the desert to be tempted by Satan. After Jesus had fasted and prayed for forty days and forty nights, the reality was, He was literally starving. At that "weak moment," the tempter came to Him and said: "If you are the Son of God, tell these stones to become bread" (Matthew 4:3). I wonder if those stones had their own flashing "Hot Now" sign. Did Jesus's mouth water? Could He imagine the scent of freshly baked bread, hot from the oven? We know what came out of Jesus's mouth, but I'm curious about what was happening in His mind.

After all, Satan spoke the truth that Jesus was, in fact, the Son of God. He absolutely could have turned those stones into the most scrumptious, warm, buttery loaf that would easily have satisfied the loud grumble of His stomach. But Jesus refused to take matters into His own hands. Instead He quoted Old Testament scripture—"It is written: 'Man shall not live on bread alone, but on every word that comes from the mouth of God'" (verse 4). He combatted the enemy's lies with truth.

As I was avoiding processing Kisha's death, I was not living by "every word that comes from the mouth of God." My ear had become more in tune with the half-truths uttered by the deceiver. Indeed, there *is* no pain in heaven. I knew with all my heart that Kisha was no longer suffering as she fellowshipped face-to-face with Jesus. That part was the truth. The lie was that the answer to *my* pain was to take my own life. But as I shut out my loved ones and spent hours and hours alone, I found it more and more difficult to separate the truth from the lies. As the enemy's voice tried to tell me how I could put an end to my problems, I thought, *Huh. That makes sense.* Without God's Word and people speaking truth to me, I began to believe the lie.

Those dark days became a miserable routine. In the morning, I would turn my head to peer at the red digital numbers revealing the time—the only light in my pitch-black room created by blackout curtains. The white noise droning from my sound machine drowned out the birds chirping outside my window. There was no point in getting up, so I would roll over, pull my comforter up to my chin, and fall back asleep. Around noon I would prop myself up with a few pillows and flip on my TV, watching drama series, crime movies, or R-rated films that fed my craving for darkness.

Around the time the sun went down, I'd head downstairs. With my muscles atrophying and back aching, I would have to place most of my weight on the railing to make the sixteen-stair descent. Once downstairs, I would plop down in my brown, upholstered recliner in front of my sixty-inch TV. With easy access to the kitchen and a multitude of delivery services available to bring whatever high-fat, high-sugar, tasty treat I desired, the binge-eating began. By midnight, with not a hint of drowsiness, I would pop two over-the-counter sleep aids and make the strenuous trek upstairs to fall asleep and start the whole cycle over again.

Those dark days blur together, but one evening I was watching a movie when a song brought back a flood of memories. As the chorus of "Lovin' You" by Minnie Riperton played in the background of a comedic scene, my mind traveled back to being on tour with Kisha. After a concert, the band and I were in the front lounge of the tour bus playing truth-or-dare. I had just completed my dare of drinking a concoction created from the many condiment packages found in the drawer of the kitchenette. With the scent of barbecue sauce, tabasco, orange juice, and some other unidentifiable scents still in the air, I called on Kisha to go next. After she hesitantly chose a dare, I issued my challenge.

"I dare you to serenade Jimmy the bus driver with 'Lovin' You.'"

With the privacy door separating the front lounge from the driver's area, our kind, unsuspecting driver had no idea what awaited him. After several minutes of stalling and clarifying how much of the song she was required to sing, Kisha sauntered to the front and sat in the passenger seat facing Jimmy. I'm sure he knew something was up as the rest of us stifled snickers and Kisha shifted nervously in the seat. It's hard to see a Black woman blush, but I'm certain Kisha's milk chocolate complexion had a strong hint of red as she launched into the seventies R&B classic love ballad. My friends and I held in our chuckles until she got to the pinnacle note that few songstresses could hit: *"La-la-la-la-la-la-la-la-la-la-la, dodn-dodn-do-do, a-a-a-a-a-AH."*

We erupted in applause and laughter, impressed that Kisha actually completed her dare and marveling at her incredible voice. She had effortlessly sailed to that high F-sharp note.

My laughter remembering the hilarity of that moment soon melted into anger over being robbed of Kisha's beautiful voice and friendship. Brennon, still a toddler, would grow up not even remembering his mom. And Kisha's older son, BJ, who was eleven when she passed, would always miss what he once had. As I wrestled again with the injustice of a forty-year-old mother of two being taken out by a disease many survived, after so many of us had prayed, the enemy's voice became louder. *It's not fair, is it?*

No, it's not, I thought. My gaze fell on the pile of empty Krispy Kreme and pizza boxes on the table next to my couch. Here I was sabotaging my body and health, but I lived on while my friend was dead. It wasn't fair. Why hadn't it been me? *No one would miss you.* The thought took root as I glanced at the bottle of sleeping pills sitting on the coffee table. If people could see me as I was right then, the last word they would associate with me would be *overcomer.* Maybe *slob* or *hypocrite* or *quitter*—but not *overcomer.* After all of my talk about healthy living and finally being victorious in the areas that had plagued me, I had hit a new low point. The very songs I was defined by now mocked me.

The lyrics from "Only the World" swirled in my head: *"Heaven is a place where the tears on every face will be wiped away. Oh, and I can't wait to go . . ."*

You don't have to wait anymore, the enemy's voice said, buttery smooth. *A handful of those pills would send you there immediately.*

I grabbed the bottle and stared at it. *How many would it take?*

As I pondered this question, I caught a glimpse of my phone sitting next to me. I'm not even sure why I had brought it downstairs. I hadn't been answering any of the calls or texts that had been flooding in. I had actively shut out my friends, but they had not forgotten about me. In fact, I had multiple voice messages from them checking up on me. My album *Out of the Dark* begins with some of the voice messages I received during my darkest days:

Hey, Dees, it's Laura. Just want you to know I'm thinking about you today and praying for you and I love you. Call me back.

Hey, Mandisa. Dave calling. Hey, I've missed not hearing from you over the last several weeks and I hope that you're all right. I want to remind you that you're a daughter of the Most High God. Love you.

Mandisa, it's Chan. I'm knocking at your door right now. Can you open your door and let me in if you're home? Just wanted to check on you to make sure you're okay.

I may have thought I was sitting there alone that night, but a spiritual battle was raging around me. And though I hadn't responded to a single one of those voice-mails, God heard my friends' prayers and used their messages. Seeing my phone, I thought about them. How long would it take for people to call the police after not hearing from me? Weeks? Months, maybe? Would the pills cause me to vomit all over myself? Who would find me, and what grisly scene might greet them? I admit, my first thoughts were of myself—how embarrassing it would be for my friends to find me like that. But my thoughts soon turned to the pain *they* would feel if I did what I was contemplating—a pain similar to what I felt from losing Kisha.

Maybe you have a friend or a loved one who is dealing with depression or anxiety, and you wonder if your calls and texts make a difference. I want to tell you, they do. When my friend Chandra knocked on my door during this period, I didn't answer. But I heard it. If my friends hadn't reached out, I probably would have listened to that lying voice of the enemy, saying, *No one is going to miss you.* My friends' consistency in reaching out to me—even when some of them were walking through valleys of their own, as I would later find out—made all the difference. You may not feel like your efforts are doing a thing, but don't give up! God is using you in a powerful way, even through the simple act of calling someone or sending a message.

Maybe *you* are the one going through a dark season right now, where you feel hopeless and alone. If you are, let me tell you about God's grace and the power of community. First, God is with you. His Word says He "is close to the brokenhearted and saves those who are crushed in spirit" (Psalm 34:18). You may not *feel* that He is there, but His presence is more than a fleeting feeling. Some things are true whether you feel them or not. Second, He wants you to connect with others. Sometimes when you least want to be with people is when it is most important to do so. God did not create you to be alone. In the Garden of Eden, God looked at Adam and said, "It is not good for the man to be alone. I will make a helper suitable for him" (Genesis 2:18). I used to think of this statement in terms of romantic relationships and marriage. And while that was the original context, many of us are single.

As of 2018, the US census revealed that around half of adults in the United States are unmarried.[2]

That's part of the reason I'm passionate about singles issues. God has so much to say about how we are to walk in relationship with others. So many of the lessons in the New Testament come down to this: Love God; love others. *Love.* Love your family, your friends, and even your enemies. Loving others is the way the world will know we are God's followers. And that kind of love isn't just for married people. I long to be married one day, but I've also decided I won't live my life "alone" until then. The people I surround myself with are so important to my mental and spiritual health. In fact, a few years ago, in an effort to make community a top priority, I decided to move across town to live in the area most of my friends live. Now I live within a few miles of most of my tribe. If they don't hear from me for a few days, much to my chagrin, they come knocking at my door!

At my lowest point, God used the words of my friends to pull me back from what could have been the worst decision of my life. As I thought about those people who cared for me, I didn't want to be the one who put them through sadness or grief. A part of me knew that I mattered, even just to these few people. My loved ones never let me go. At the time, I had no idea how hard they were fighting for me. But I would soon learn the depths of their love and how far they were willing to go to help me.

INTERVENTION

Shortly after my low point, which I sometimes refer to as "the deep dark," I realized that if I were going to stick around, I would need to start working again to pay the bills. I reluctantly agreed to go on the Rock & Worship Roadshow Tour. It had been a long time since my band and I had been together, so we needed to rehearse. I didn't want to be there, but I had no choice. I had not released any new music in three years, so we had performed these songs countless times. After a few hours of doing the bare minimum, I desperately wanted to get out of that rehearsal space. Since this was the first time I had left my house, I took advantage of being out and decided to trade in my recliner for the recliner seats at Regal Cinemas and treat myself to a movie.

I hadn't been to a movie theater in months, but I wanted to see *War Room*, a Christian film that featured my song "Press On." At the theater, I sat down with my overflowing bucket of popcorn, excited to see my song play on the big screen. In the film, Tony and Elizabeth—played by Priscilla Shirer—have a strained marriage that's falling apart. Elizabeth is a Realtor and one of her clients, Miss Clara, encourages her to turn her closet into a "war room," where she can pray for help amid the battles she's facing. By the end of the movie, everyone's saved, restored, and thriving. I left the theater feeling annoyed and angry. In my experience, "happily ever after" happened in scripts, not reality. It certainly wasn't *my* reality—or Kisha's.

Something else was going on too. I was offended by the light. John 3:20 says, "Everyone who does evil hates the light, and will not come into the light for fear that their deeds will be exposed." When you're surrounding yourself with darkness, the littlest amount of light can be painful. But light makes the darkness flee. Ephesians 5:8 says, "For you were once darkness, but now you are light in the Lord. Live as children of light."

In the time that had passed since Kisha's death, I hadn't been doing that. I had been living life my own way—in darkness. So that movie was like an annoying bright light shining in my eyes. I felt uncomfortable and exposed. I was so angry and upset that I wanted a second movie to cleanse my palate. I remember thinking I didn't want to go home with that "everything works for good" message on my heart. *I need to get this Christianese stuff out of my spirit,* I thought.

By the time the second movie ended, I had been inside that theater for over four hours. When I walked out into the parking lot, I noticed something strange about my red Toyota Solara. I squinted my eyes. The light speckles all over the car were yellow sticky notes! As I got closer, I was able to read what they said:

We love you.

We miss you.

Come back to us.

Some of the notes had scriptures written on them. When I looked up, I saw several of my friends getting out of their cars. They had been waiting for me for four hours! My friend Laura, who had organized the intervention, had gone to my house earlier and become convinced I was home but ignoring her incessant knocking. My offhanded mention of my movie plans to my keyboard player, Jon, became a clue to Inspector Laura as to my whereabouts. I later discovered that my friends had driven to several theaters in town until they found my car. They'd covered it with their sticky-note encouragements and then waited until the movie was over. They hadn't expected me to watch two films!

At first I was annoyed. They had invaded my privacy.

"What are you doing here?" I snapped, a scowl on my face. "How did you find me?" My friends were like little lightbulbs walking around, and their brightness was uncomfortable.

"We just want to sit and talk with you for a few minutes," Laura said. "This has been going on for too long."

"No! I'm going home!"

"Disa," Tammy said gently. "Please. Just a few minutes."

I knew they weren't going to leave me alone until I agreed. "Fine, whatever." The looks of sorrow and concern on their faces made me feel horrible.

They had already picked out an outdoor area beside the Panera Bread next door. My friends circled around me for an intervention. Each of them took a turn telling me what I meant to them and ending with why they were concerned with the present state of affairs. I don't know if you've ever been on the receiving end of an intervention, but it's not pleasant. I couldn't be angry at them because of their kindness, but I was annoyed at their interference. *Light.*

"We love you."

"We can't let you keep doing this."

"We're fighting for you."

One of my friends said, "Disa, we love you just the way you are." I'd heard those words before, and my friend could tell I was beginning to check out. But she continued, "No, hear this. We want you to know we love you just the way you are. But we love you too much to leave you there." That felt like God speaking directly to me.

I could hear Him saying, "I will take you at four hundred pounds and love you no matter how much you weigh and how much you try to push Me away. But I love you too much to leave you in that place."

Finally, after everyone had said their piece, with my walls still up but not quite as formidable, I asked, "What do you want me to do?"

They told me they wanted me to get counseling, and Dan had already found someone I could meet with. I agreed to it, maybe just to get them off my back, or maybe knowing I needed professional help. Either way, that uncomfortable, awkward, embarrassing alfresco meeting was a turning point. The darkness felt a little less dark. I could see a small flicker. Light was beginning to break through.

Getting Real

- When you're going through hard times, to what or to whom do you turn for comfort?
- Have you ever pushed God away? What did this look like?

- Satan can be a crafty adversary. Have you ever been tricked by His lies about you or your circumstances? What happened?
- In what ways is Christian community essential in our everyday lives? What are some ways you can cultivate healthy friendships?
- Who do you know who might need some "sticky note" encouragement today? Make a plan to reach out.

eight

I'M STILL HERE

I know it's been a while
Since anybody's seen me smilin'
Shame had me thinking it was game over
Thought my best days were gone, yeah
Turns out that I was wrong
'Cause this is my comeback song
And by the grace of God
I'm still here!

My friends' intervention jolted me back to the reality of where my choices were leading me. I immediately made good on my promise to see the counselor they recommended. I worked with her for a couple of months, and while those sessions helped to begin the process, that counselor wasn't the right fit for me. To be fair, I was in such a rough place that anybody would have had a hard time breaking through the wall I had put up.

What I really wanted was a therapist who shared my beliefs. So many of my issues were intertwined with my faith. Having someone who understood what I was experiencing from more than a clinical standpoint would put me at ease. Danielle, my current counselor, came highly recommended by a friend. Not only did she have a strong faith in God, but also she specialized in touring musicians, so she understood many of my specific struggles. In the early days of the COVID-19 pandemic, she did something no other therapist had ever done. After admitting to her that I was canceling our afternoon session because I didn't want to talk about my feelings, she asked if she could pray for me. Reading the prayer she texted me was like a flicker of light among gathering storm clouds. Danielle respected my boundaries but could also stand up to me; she wouldn't let me push her away.

In our early sessions, she gave me a tool to help me process the grief and shame I still often experience. When I wrestle with a particular feeling, Danielle encourages me to create a scene in my mind where I can take those negative emotions. Some people imagine a warm beach in Tahiti or a tranquil, candlelit bubble bath. But when

Danielle asks me to envision a place that makes me feel safe, protected, and content, I picture the tomb of Jesus.

If you were to listen in on one of my sessions with Danielle, you might hear her say, "Let's take this to the tomb." Here's what that looks like: I walk up to the tomb with the stone laid across the entrance. With a mere push of my hand, the stone rolls away, and I am face-to-face with Jesus. He sits on the stony bench but jumps up when I enter, smiling as if He has never been happier to see anyone. I long to run to His outstretched arms but am kept in place by the weight of the shame, anger, insecurity, or other negative feeling I am carrying.

"Can I take that for you?" Jesus has a peaceful look in His eye. I then heave the negativity—which has taken on the form of a heavy medicine ball—into the dark corner of the tomb. I feel lighter already, but the exchange isn't finished. I kneel in front of my Savior while He gently lays seven colored scarves around my neck. One at a time He clothes me with compassion, kindness, humility, gentleness, patience, forbearance, and forgiveness. He then binds the vivid rainbow of scarves with a beautiful gold medallion shaped like a heart and representing love.

I'm reminded of the words of Colossians 3:12–14. They assure me that I am "holy and dearly loved" and am to clothe myself with virtues and love, "which binds them all together in perfect unity."

Jesus pulls me to my feet, and I thank Him with a big hug. The first time I went to the tomb, I turned around to walk out but something felt wrong about that. I quickly turned around and sheepishly said, "I don't want to turn my back on You, Jesus." The chuckle He stifled as I backed out of the tomb always makes me think of how much He enjoys me. With a promise to return to spend time with Him soon, I roll the stone back over the entrance and skip away feeling lighter than ever before. This technique helps me make the choice to leave the heaviness I often carry at the feet of Jesus.

SHAME OFF

In the year and a half since Kisha's death, I had gained two hundred pounds. I had fallen away from the healthy habits I once nurtured. For me, food issues have always been tied to shame. Over and over, I have felt like I don't measure up because of that struggle. I didn't feel deserving of God's help in getting me out of the same hole I'd dug myself into again. And yet, I was too weak to climb out by myself. What I didn't understand then was how desperately He loved me and wanted to help me.

Learning to accept who I am and clothe myself in God's righteousness is not an easy process for someone so accustomed to wearing the dark cloak of shame. I remember feeling ashamed as a child when a classmate or family member made a comment about my weight. I instantly felt unworthy because I didn't meet their standard. That terrible feeling would lead me to cut myself off from people and eat—only making the initial issue worse because it caused me to gain even more weight. Shame is a painful emotion that says, "You don't measure up. You are a failure." In one way, none of us measures up. Romans 3:23 says, "For all have sinned and fall short of the glory of God." You may fail in different ways than I do, but we all fail to perfectly keep God's commands. None of us stacks up to God's holiness, and realizing that reality can lead to shame.

Shame not only drives a wedge between us and the Father; it can also drive a wedge between us and others. When the Bible says we don't measure up, it's talking about our sinful natures. Nobody lives a perfect life. I think that's pretty apparent when we look at the world around us. Sin separates us from a Holy God. Coming to Him through Christ requires that we recognize our guilt, confess our sin, and turn from it to follow Him.

Guilt is different from shame. Guilt is seeing the sinful thing you have done; shame is seeing yourself as a failure because of it. The difference between the two is a fine line I have always struggled to maintain. I have often felt like a failure because of my sin—and at times just for who I was or how I failed to meet others' expectations. But shame is toxic, and God doesn't want it to hinder His work in my life. One of the benefits of being His child is that the work of Christ lifts my shame! I'm still learning this—and it's a lesson I imagine I'll spend a lifetime learning. But verses like Isaiah 50:7 have encouraged me: "Because the Sovereign LORD helps me, I will not be disgraced. Therefore have I set my face like flint, and I know I will not be put to shame." Shame is not God's way. It is one of the things that holds me in darkness. When I came to God again after pushing Him away, I felt so embarrassed. *I can't come to You in this condition,* I would think.

One day, I was listening to K-LOVE Christian radio, something I'd completely stopped doing, when I heard the song "One Step Away" by Casting Crowns. The words floated out of my car speakers and hit me like a ton of bricks. I felt like God was saying, "You don't have to fix yourself, Mandisa. Just turn around. I'm right here." Even though I knew I hadn't been living the way God wanted me to, He reassured my heart that He was waiting patiently one step away. It wasn't a wide chasm I had to scale; I simply had to turn to Him and fall into His welcoming embrace.

In Luke 15 Jesus tells the story of a father and two sons. The older brother was really into rules and did everything by the book. The younger son was wild and asked his father for his part of the inheritance early. In Jewish culture, that was a big no-no and the equivalent of telling your dad you wished he were dead. But the father gave his younger son the money he requested, with no hassle. The young man left home and squandered his wealth in foolish living—girls, booze, and partying. When his money was gone, there was a famine in the land, and to survive, he took a job caring for pigs. This was an unbelievably humiliating job for a Jewish person, because his culture considered pork to be unclean. But the true low point was when the young man was so hungry he longed to eat the food the pigs were eating.

Having arrived at rock bottom, the man finally realized he'd be better off as a servant for his dad than in his current position. So he headed home, hoping that maybe his dad would allow him to join the household staff. There's this beautiful scene where the father sees his son from a great distance and runs to him, embraces him, and kisses him. The son delivers an impassioned speech, telling his dad that he has sinned against him and declaring his unworthiness to be his son. Without batting an eye, the father has his servants dress the young man in a fine robe. They put a ring on his finger and sandals on his feet. Then the father throws a big party to celebrate. "For this son of mine was dead and is alive again; he was lost and is found," the father says (Luke 15:24).

I have always loved the story of the prodigal son. It's a beautiful picture of the love of the Father in spite of our failings. In the story, the father doesn't heap shame on his wayward son; in fact, he does just the opposite. He welcomes him back with open arms and celebrates him. *Wow.* It blows me away to know that's how God feels about me. No matter how many times I fail and dig myself into that same hole, my heavenly Father celebrates when I return to Him. Still, coming out of darkness when you've been hanging out in that place for a while is a process. I love that all the son did was come back to the father—and the father ran to him. But think about the son's journey back from the pigsty. It probably felt like a long walk. With each step, the son must have speculated at what his father's response would be. Maybe he was like me and mentally rehearsed how he would respond to each objection raised.

When I decided to turn around, it felt like a slow trudge, one foot in front of the other. My heavenly Father's forgiveness was instant, but my restoration wasn't immediate. I still had a long way to go.

THE LONG ROAD BACK

At the beginning of 2016, I joined Jeremy Camp, Danny Gokey, and other artists on the Rock & Worship Roadshow. Every concert was really difficult—some of the hardest performances of my life. Moving onstage was difficult with the extra weight I was carrying. I'd do a set of four or five songs and have to be seated for half of it. Sweat poured down my face, and my back hurt after every concert. I sang my most well-known songs, "Good Morning," "Stronger," and "Overcomer" to grateful crowds who cheered loudly. I had just started talking *to* God again, but at every performance I still had to get onstage and talk *about* Him.

At one concert, in a packed stadium in California, I sat on a stool after singing "Stronger," which proclaims that God is going to use your hardships. The song says that God's right there even if it's hard to see Him. I thought about all I'd been through the past few years. I needed to hear those words as much as my audience did. I quoted 1 Peter 5:10, which says, "And the God of all grace, who called you to his eternal glory in Christ, after you have suffered a little while, will himself restore you and make you strong, firm and steadfast."

"Let me tell you," I began. "When Peter was writing that, he was writing to those who say, 'I am a follower of Jesus Christ.' Sometimes we walk through things that we feel are going to take us out. I am a living witness of that. But here's what I also know: If you're still here on earth, if there is still breath in your body, then God has given you everything you need to take the very next step." The stadium erupted in cheers.

"There's some of you here tonight that need to be reminded to hold on a little bit longer. The pain won't last forever. You are going to have a story that will pull someone else out of the pit you're currently in. True redemption, which God the Father specializes in, is when God uses the thing you're not sure you can make it through and makes it your ministry."

At that point, I was preaching to myself as much as to the audience. With God's help, I was beginning to climb out of that pit. I tried to be as honest as I could and not sugar-coat the hard things I and others might be going through. I found that being honest about my own pain ministered to people. It gave them permission to wrestle with their own questions and hurts.

On tour, I was able to talk with some of the other artists, who are true believers with deep faith. One of those was Jeremy Camp. He had also lost someone he loved to cancer. His first wife, Melissa, had died of ovarian cancer less than a year after they married. I asked him questions like "How do you trust God?" and "How do you still pray in faith, knowing you prayed so hard for her healing and God said no?"

Hearing how songs like "I Still Believe" came from these difficult seasons of struggle encouraged me. Knowing that deep soul-wrenching had led Jeremy to make declarations about believing without seeing inspired me to do the same. I longed for that kind of faith, but was I willing to wrestle with God? Or would I keep shutting Him out instead? Combining our two experiences with sorrow, Jeremy and I wrote a song together about walking in unwavering faith: "My First Love" was an honest reflection of where I was:

> How long will I forget You?
> And how long will I pretend that You're not here?

And it was a hopeful declaration of where I wanted to be:

I wanna go back to where it all began
I wanna go past the walls that hold me in
To trust what I know
Feel You so close
I can hear Your heartbeat
I wanna go back, back to my first love

Another artist on tour with us, Danny Gokey, had also lost his wife. Danny, who placed third on season eight of *American Idol*, auditioned for the show four weeks after his wife, Sophia, died from complications during heart surgery. She had been the one who had encouraged him to audition, and he wanted to honor her memory and tell her story. I was encouraged by Danny's belief that God could still be trusted.

Looking back, it's uncanny the people God put me on tour with at such a pivotal time in my life. Light pushed through the darkness every time I heard Danny and Jeremy talk about how they persevered in faith with broken hearts. I would expect it to be impossible to trust God after losing their spouses through tragic circumstances, and yet they did. In the midst of pain and loss, they chose to keep believing. In spite of losing someone they loved, these men abided in the love of Christ and continued to proclaim God's goodness. Observing their faith and strength began to heal some of the raw parts of my broken heart.

I'M STILL HERE

Testimonies are powerful. God uses our stories to encourage others and to reveal His power and goodness. It reminds me of Psalm 66:16, which says, "Come and hear, all you who fear God; let me tell you what he has done for me." When we proclaim to fellow Christians what God has done in our lives, it strengthens their faith and ours. Some of my most powerful songs have been stories of something God has done in my life. I love to proclaim from stage the victories God has accomplished in my walk with Him. And as I tell others about the ways He has been faithful, I am encouraged in return.

HOLDING ON

At the end of March 2016, I returned home following the two-month tour. Those months had been a time of healing for me, but they had also been a distraction. As I stepped back inside my house where I'd gone dark, I knew I could easily be drawn into old habits. I had taken some steps toward healing, but I still found it difficult to not return to the harmful habits that caused my spiral. Thankfully, when the steady time on the road came to an end, my community didn't let up on me. After I asked for their forgiveness for how I had treated them during "the deep dark," I chose to respond when

151

they reached out. I answered their texts and calls. I let them pray with me and share my burdens. One night a few of us were sitting around my living room, when my friend Janine, one of my background vocalists, started telling a story about something that had happened when I was in the dark. One day, she and her daughters noticed a beautiful moth on the outside of their front window. It was trying to break free from a spider's web. It flapped its wings, but the harder it tried to get away from the web, the more stuck it became. All of a sudden, they saw a big spider moving along the web, coming to devour the moth. The moth started flapping, trying to get loose. Not wanting her children to witness the moth's untimely death, Janine began frantically banging on the glass, hoping the vibration would lead to its freedom. Janine continued with her expressive voice: "The moth got free and flew away!"

She continued, "I feel like the Holy Spirit said, 'Disa.' It was a testament to me that God hears His kids, and the prayers of a righteous person avails much." As Janine told me that story, I became emotional. Almost a year had passed since that event. And during that time, Janine had traveled on the road with me when I was at my lowest. Little did I know that as I curled up in my bunk on the tour bus, Janine would be right outside my curtain, figuratively banging on the bus in prayer. God had revealed to her that the moth was me—and He wanted to set me free.

Around that time, as I worked on restoring my broken friendships, the relationship most in need of rehabilitation was my relationship with God. I was far removed from the seasons when time would fly as I spent hours in His Word and in prayer, and I struggled with the shame of what had been lost. The Holy Spirit's constant reminder to take those thoughts captive—and strategies I needed to do so—became a lifeline. Since sticky notes had become a vehicle of hope for me, I placed little reminders on my mirror, refrigerator, and bathroom scale—anywhere I went frequently. These prompts assured me with messages such as, "I am with you," "You are worthy," "Talk to Me." When my eye would catch one of these notes, I would turn my attention to the Father and have a little chat with Him. This made my time with Him feel like less of a "to-do list," and more like a relationship.

I found myself enjoying my time in the Word again. Starting my day with a devotional plan from the YouVersion Bible app or Proverbs 31 Ministries' First Five app launched my scripture reading. Sometimes the passages I heard on Sunday at church would strike a chord in my heart, and I would choose to study those further. I began recognizing God's voice again. It wasn't the voice I had been listening to that had led me to a place of shame. No, this voice was full of joy, peace, and hope. He assured me that He was not done with me yet. The best was yet to come.

Like that moth Janine freed from the web, God freed me from the darkness. Psalm 40:1–3 became my heart's cry:

> I waited patiently for the LORD;
> he turned to me and heard my cry.
> He lifted me out of the slimy pit,
> out of the mud and mire;
> he set my feet on a rock
> and gave me a firm place to stand.
> He put a new song in my mouth,
> A hymn of praise to our God.
> Many will see and fear the LORD
> and put their trust in him.

I was about to discover the new song He had for me to sing. Though I hadn't encountered the specific strategy yet, I was learning to "take it to the tomb." And someone close to me, someone I had nearly given up on, was about to surprise me with his own journey from darkness to light.

Getting Real

- Have you ever felt like you had to "fix yourself" before you could come to God? What happened?
- What does Jesus's story of the prodigal son show us about our heavenly Father? What does it reveal about our own journey back to God?
- I was impacted by the stories of Jeremy Camp and Danny Gokey. How have you been impacted by another believer's story? How has your story affected someone else?
- Do you have a "testimony" of God's goodness that someone else needs to hear?
- Prayer, reading scripture, and attending church are all ways to "feed on light." How are you incorporating these three things into your life? Do you need to add more?

nine

PROVE ME WRONG

Would it be wrong if I asked You for proof?
I wish that I could just believe without questioning
I'm just being honest with You
And they say Your ways are better
But I still don't understand
And You can't hold me together
And this can't be Your perfect plan

P rove Me Wrong" was the first song I wrote after
Kisha died. I began the verse talking to God about
Kisha specifically: "You could've healed her. You've done
it before. You could've sent the angels down and turned it
around. Wouldn't that have meant so much more?"

I was finally voicing some of the hard questions I had
for God. In the two years since Kisha had died, I had

stuffed my emotions, pulling back from my faith. I had used food, TV, and other things to comfort myself, but they had only made me more depressed and angry. I was finally ready to get real with God about how I was feeling and how I was hurting.

Since Kisha's death, a part of me had tried to hide my negative emotions from God. After all, wasn't it disrespectful to question Him? Over time, I began to see that He already knew everything I was feeling—good and bad. When given the choice between fight or flight, my default has always been flight: ignore and avoid the pain at all costs. I know I'm not the only one who does this, because God doesn't gloss over the not-so-good tendencies of the people we read about in His Word.

In fact, I'm pretty sure that when I get to heaven, King David and I will be good friends. Since we'll be in our glorified bodies, we won't have the distractions that accompany our penchants for moodiness or cravings of the flesh. Maybe we'll write songs together. I imagine our heavenly homes being the sites of many banquets, dance parties, and movie nights. In my theater room, equipped with a big screen and recliner seats, I can show him what was happening in the spiritual realm when I forgave Simon. We can follow that up by projecting how the heavenlies were joining the celebration as David danced before the ark of the Lord in 2 Samuel 6. I know we don't have the exact details of what heaven will be like, but I imagine David and I will get along.

When I read about David's life, triumphs, mistakes, and expressions to God, I can relate on so many levels. He wrote many of the psalms in scripture, and when you start to read them, you quickly see that his emotions were *all over the place.* He asks:

"Why have You forsaken me?"

"Where are You, God?"

"Why do You let the wicked flourish?"

In one of my favorites, Psalm 13, David starts by asking the Lord how long He will forget him. Will it be *forever?* But four short verses later, David is rejoicing and singing, full of trust and confidence in God. He expresses anger, lament, praise, sorrow, joy, shame, and awe— sometimes in the same psalm. I love how David tells it like it is. He knows he can't hide it from God anyway, so he just lets it out. And as he does, he creates space for God to correct false thinking with the truth, letting the light shine in on his flawed perspective.

Acts 13:22 says these amazing words about David spoken by God: "I have found David son of Jesse, a man after my own heart; he will do everything I want him to do." Even with his wild, up-and-down emotions (and serious slipups), David is called a man after God's own heart. At times I'm tempted to hide my negative emotions. But I think when we talk to God about our doubts, hurts, and disappointments, He speaks more clearly into our darkness. Sometimes His voice is the loudest in our pain. Christian apologist C.S. Lewis wrote: "Pain insists upon being attended to. God whispers to us in our pleasures, speaks in our conscience, but shouts in our pain: it is His megaphone to rouse a deaf world."[3]

I've discovered that when I let God into my deepest struggles, my questions may increase, but so does my intimacy with Him. Do you ever remember being angry with a parent when you were a kid? Maybe your mom or dad told you no when you wanted to hear yes. But no matter how angry you were with your parents, they didn't stop loving you.

During my Living Proof Live days, I would spend a lot of time with Travis Cottrell and his family. I have a vivid memory of seeing Travis discipline his then seven-year-old son, Jack. After the tantrum was over and Jack had received his consequence, Travis did something that left an indelible mark on me. He pulled his crying son close and set him on his lap. He took him into his arms and reassured him of his love. From my fly-on-the-wall perspective, I saw that any cracks trying to form in the foundation of their relationship were filled with love rather than shame.

The same is true with our heavenly Father. When we cry out to Him in our pain, He is right there ready to wrap His arms around us—even when we are experiencing His discipline. Psalm 34:18 puts it like this: "The LORD is close to the brokenhearted and saves those who are crushed in spirit." When we are at our lowest, God is right there with us. Jesus echoed this sentiment in the Sermon on the Mount when He said, "Blessed are the poor in spirit, for theirs is the kingdom of heaven" (Matthew 5:3). The way we truly experience God is when we let Him in—not only on our best days but also on our worst.

Many of the songs I wrote for my album *Out of the Dark* delved into my doubts and questions about things that had happened in my life. I wondered if songs like "Prove Me Wrong"—where I asked God to prove to me that His ways are best—would be well-received by my listeners. The songs weren't my trademark upbeat, encouraging power anthems. Would Christian radio stations play songs that addressed racial injustice ("Bleed the Same"), spiritual doubts ("My First Love"), and fighting for hope ("I'm Still Here")? The truth was, it didn't matter. God was using these songs—and me writing and singing them—to bring me further out of the dark.

I recently read the story of a writer whose twenty-year-old son passed away unexpectedly. After raising his son to love God, the father felt like the rug had been ripped out from under his feet. He talked about feeling afraid of God—not only a respect of His abilities and sovereignty, but also a fear of how God might exercise those abilities. "It was, after all, just a month ago that God exercised his sovereignty in taking my son to himself," the man wrote on his blog. "My life of ease and privilege was interrupted by a loss so great I would never have allowed myself to even imagine it. In one moment God delivered a blow that staggered me, that very nearly crushed me."[4]

That's how I felt when Kisha died. It was as if God had pulled the rug out from under me. I knew God was sovereign, but I grappled with a good God allowing such bad things to happen to those He loved. Didn't He know how much pain it would cause those who loved Kisha? Didn't He know how I'd respond? The answer is *yes*. He knew. But He allowed it anyway. That's what I had to come to terms with. That God was "compassionate and gracious, slow to anger, abounding in love" (Psalm 103:8). And painful circumstances in my life did not make that untrue.

CRY FOR HELP

The baby steps I was taking back to trusting God were propelled by something surprising. On July 10, 2016, I woke up to a string of missed calls and a voicemail message from my brother John. The moment I heard his shaky voice on the recording, I knew something was wrong. He told me he was okay, but the news he shared next caused me to freeze in fear. On the voicemail, he told me he had been shot. I gasped and hit the callback button. As the phone rang, I was reminded of another time I had heard John's shaky voice over the phone.

Ten years earlier, John and his girlfriend had been expecting a baby. This child would be my mom's first grandchild, and while she never said so, I suspected she was excited. The baby girl was born with a heart defect, and she remained at the hospital with wires and sensors attached to her tiny body.

My brother and I didn't talk much about faith in those days, so I was surprised when he called me up and asked me to pray for his little girl. I worked at Lifeway at the time, and my life was Bible studies and Christian resources, so I was full of faith about what God would do. I believed God would not only heal my niece but also use the experience to draw John to Himself. Rather than simply pray *for* John, I longed to pray *with* him. That night, I spoke a bold prayer over the phone. I prayed that God would completely heal John's infant daughter. I asked the Great Physician to breathe life into her lungs and cause her heart to beat steadily. I remember thinking, *Father, this is Your opportunity! When You heal his baby, John is going to know that You're real, that You're alive, and that You do powerful things.* As I prayed over the phone that night, I felt the power and presence of the Holy Spirit. I thought I knew how He would answer. But I was wrong.

A few days later, the baby died.

My faith was shaken. I thought that when God answered my prayer, my brother would want a relationship with Him. When the baby died, I felt like God had messed up. *This was Your chance, God!* I thought. *This could have been the moment.* I'd been able to move forward from that loss, but I hadn't understood God's ways or His plan. I would have done things differently if I had been in charge. Thank God, I am not!

DEAR JOHN

Over the years, there have been multiple times when I have pleaded with God for my brother's salvation. I even wrote about it in the song "Dear John":

> There's freedom
> On the other side of
> Things that keep us tied up and afraid
> There's hope in every situation
> No matter what you're facing every day
> But it's up to you
> You get to choose
> Your Father is waiting there with open arms
> Dear John

One of my deepest desires was for my brother to spend eternity in heaven with me. I spoke about it often to friends, in interviews, and on social media. My friend and one of my favorite singers, Natalie Grant, even set a reminder on her phone to pray for John's salvation. After Kisha's death, as my faith was waning, God still heard the petitions of the righteous pounding the gates of heaven on John's behalf. I hadn't spoken to God about John in quite a while, but as my brother picked up the phone and retold the story of how close he came to death, I understood the importance of that moment.

There is something about life-or-death situations that cause people to look up. Lying in the hospital, John told me all about the previous night and how his life had flashed before his eyes. He ended his story by saying he believed he was alive because of all the prayers that had been lifted up for him. I reminded my brother of some of the lyrics I had written about him years ago:

> It's not a list of dos and don'ts
> Not a record of your faults
> He gave His life to pay it all
> Dear John
> He loves you just the way you are
> You are forgiven by His scars
> Just open up your heart

I asked if he were ready to open up his heart and let Jesus in. Like so many times in the past, he told me he wasn't ready yet. But something in his hesitation made me think he might be close. Without pushing, I asked him to call me when he was ready. I hung up and for the first time in a while, I pleaded with God for my brother's salvation. I thanked Him for sparing John's life and felt a hope spark within me. At the same time, memories of unanswered prayers from the past welled up. I needed backup.

A few nights later, I invited my friends Janine, Amy, and Sheryl to my house to watch a movie. We watched

Miracles from Heaven, another faith-based movie that ends happily ever after. When the film ended, I felt that familiar irritation, but a mustard seed of faith prompted my next move. I asked my friends to pray for John. I figured that if I were the problem because I wasn't in a good enough place to be heard by God, I didn't want that to hinder my brother from coming to Christ. (I see now how flawed that thinking was; it had zero percent to do with me and everything to do with God's grace and mercy.)

After my friends left, I was still brooding over the movie—a true story that involved a miraculous healing. The same old questions popped up in my mind: How does God choose what narrative He writes for what person? Does *how* I pray impact the outcome? What about *how many* people pray? Why does one person die and another live?

These musings were getting a bit too heavy and theological for me, so I jumped in my car and drove to the nearest fast-food drive-thru to escape my own thoughts. Little did I know that as I sat at the Hardee's intercom, about to order the largest, fattiest, most sugar-filled escape route from my hard emotions, my friends were in their car, praying for my brother.

Just then, my phone rang. "Disa," John said quietly. "You said to call you when I was ready. I think I'm ready."

I was caught off guard. There I was, running away from the voice of God at the drive-thru window, and here He was, invading my escape plan! At that moment, the Hardee's worker's voice echoed over the intercom, asking for my order. I told John I was out and would call him in a few minutes when I got home. As I ordered my double-thick cheeseburger, onion rings, and large strawberry milkshake, I knew I should not have gotten off the phone with John.

The spiritual warfare swirling around both my brother and me in that moment was strong. Sitting in line, I texted my three friends, telling them John had called and asking them to pray. Filled with anticipation about what might happen, but worried about messing things up, I started praying. I couldn't shake the feeling that I should not wait to talk to my brother. So when I was handed my order, I pulled into one of the parking spots at Hardee's and dialed John's number. I definitely didn't think I was in the best place to lead my brother to Christ, but I had a mustard seed of faith and was willing to offer that up to the Lord.

"That was fast!" John said when he answered the phone. I explained that I had a feeling I needed to call him back *now*. He chuckled and explained that my feeling was correct. He had started to doubt. After he asked me a few questions about what was about to happen and what would be required of him, I asked if he were ready. Somehow I stuttered through the plan of salvation—admitting sin, believing Jesus died and rose again to pay the penalty for sin, and accepting Jesus's free gift of eternal life. All the scriptures I needed were hidden in my heart, though they were a bit dusty. When I invited him to repeat the prayer after me, I heard my strong, rugged brother burst into tears. A few minutes later, my brother entered the family of Christ and became my brother for the second time.

I still find it amazing that when I was just barely talking to God, He gave me the sacred privilege of leading John to Christ—something I had been praying for, for years. God is so strategic! His timing—the night of June 13, 2016—meant that event not only drew my brother to Himself but also drew me closer to Him. As I rejoiced in my brother's salvation, I thought, *You knew all along, God. I'm sorry I questioned You.* Praying with my brother made me realize God does hear my prayers, even when I'm praying them out of a dark place. He hears.

God used that experience to bolster my faith and inspire the song "Good News." I mean, think about it: We live in a world that is full of bad news—pandemics, natural disasters, broken relationships, and struggling families. It's easy to focus on everything that's going wrong and forget that we have good news. When we see something happen that only God can do, we need to proclaim it to others. Isaiah 52:7 paints a beautiful picture: "How beautiful on the mountains are the feet of those who bring good news, who proclaim peace, who bring good tidings, who proclaim salvation, who say to Zion, 'Your God reigns!'" Nothing in this world brings as much joy and happiness as recognizing how great and powerful God is and sharing the good news of salvation with others.

John accepting Christ as His Savior was a turning point for me. I continued to pour out my heart to the Lord in the songs I wrote and sang for *Out of the Dark*. The album was my most raw and honest, and when it was released, I suddenly had the opportunity to talk about hard issues like depression, food addiction, and mental health. I went on radio shows and even *Good Morning America* to talk about the darkness I'd experienced following Kisha's death. There was a four-year hiatus between my previous album and this one, and part of me wondered if there were still a place for me in making music. This album voiced some things that felt taboo, particularly in Christian circles. So I was surprised when so many people related to my struggles and doubts. Many of them told me my story encouraged them because it helped them to know they were not alone. Writing the songs for *Out of the Dark* opened up many unexpected and important conversations about the messiness of walking with Jesus. And while I wondered if my honesty would get me kicked out of Christian music, God had other ideas. And I was about to see how much bigger and better His plans were than my own.

Getting Real

- Have you had difficulty expressing your honest emotions to God? How does King David's experience encourage you?
- Have you ever felt afraid of God and what He might do? What are some ways you can build greater trust in God's goodness?
- I was encouraged when my brother John received the gift of salvation. Have you ever experienced an answer to prayer that strengthened your faith? What happened?
- "It's easy to focus on everything that's going wrong and forget that we have good news. When we see

OUT OF THE DARK

something happen that only God can do, we need to proclaim it to others." Talk about a time when you proclaimed the good news to others.

- Going through a difficult season can open up opportunities to have important conversations. How have you seen God use your pain and hardship for His glory and your good?

172

ten

BLEED THE SAME

We all bleed the same
We're more beautiful when we come together
We all bleed the same
So tell me why, tell me why
We're divided

The beginning of 2020 was one of the best starts to a new year I had experienced. I attended Onsite, an emotional wellness retreat, for a four-day intensive that focused on inner healing from trauma. Healthy eating and exercising had once again become a consistent part of my life, and I was thriving physically. My spiritual life flourished too. I had a healthy appetite for God's Word and communing with His Spirit. I was finding balance in my relationships as I hosted online Bible studies in my new apartment in Franklin, Tennessee. I was even loving life on the road as part of the Greatness of Our God Tour with the Newsboys. Then, in mid-March, everything came to a screeching halt.

With the global coronavirus pandemic hitting the US, show after show was postponed and then cancelled. Our tour buses took up residence back in Tennessee for the foreseeable future. And I holed up in my apartment. Knowing my tendency to "go dark" when I spend too much time alone, I reached out to my close friends and asked them to hold me accountable to stay in community. We planned group FaceTime chats, Zoom brunches, and regular phone calls to stay connected.

In addition to the pandemic, 2020 was also an election year, which further divided people. Tensions were already high, with much of the world tuning in to media outlets more than ever. And that spring, the murders of George Floyd, Ahmaud Arbery, and Breonna Taylor garnered a level of attention I had never seen before. I have always grieved when these tragedies occur, but in the past, Black Americans had been the leading voices responding to such incidents. This time I noticed many outside the Black community were speaking out.

As people around the country responded with protests, rallies, and social media posts, a couple of music executives organized "Blackout Tuesday," calling for a collective response to protest racism and police brutality. On June 2, I and many of my fellow musicians posted a black box on social media with the hashtag #theshowmustbepaused. I posted not to support a particular movement but to raise awareness for the concerns and feelings of Black people in our country, me included.

As a Black woman, I was moved by the supportive comments from friends and fans who committed to joining me in praying for change. I felt seen, validated, and hopeful that better days were on the horizon. As that hope was starting to well up in my heart, I scrolled through the comments sections of a few of my fellow CCM artists, who had also posted the black box. As I did, those warm feelings of hope quickly turned cold. Insults and criticism flew like icicle daggers. It appeared some people were more willing to speak their minds in response to the posts of my paler brothers and sisters than to mine. The criticism and bold offense of believers toward one another broke my heart.

I know this issue is complex. I'm not here to argue the political nuances of racial injustice. I can only speak from my personal experiences. I have been on the receiving end of blatant racial jabs, and I've experienced moments where I felt maligned because of my skin color. That is why it means so much to me that God often speaks about justice and defending the underdog in His Word. Isaiah 1:17 says, "Learn to do right; seek justice. Defend the oppressed. Take up the cause of the fatherless; plead the case of the widow."

We may differ on what this verse implies or on the mechanics of carrying it out, but as Christians, there's no getting around the fact that we are to seek justice and correct injustice when given the opportunity. Our God loves justice, but He is also the God of mercy. He sees the oppressed in every corner of this world He created. Regardless of individual beliefs, each Christian is called to look to the Lord for justice.

Unfortunately, what I noticed during summer 2020 was how this issue of racial injustice seemed to tear apart and divide society and even Christians. In Galatians, Paul told believers, "There is neither Jew nor Gentile, neither slave nor free, nor is their male and female, for you are all one in Christ Jesus" (Galatians 3:28). We are all on the same team: Team Jesus. And part of being "one in Christ Jesus" is seeking to understand one another and showing compassion when our brothers and sisters are in pain. We emulate our heavenly Father when we "rise up and show compassion" to those in need of justice.

Christian author Randy Alcorn recounts that he read eighty books about African American history while doing research for his novel *Dominion* (one of my all-time favorites). Doing this radically changed his perspective on the dynamics of racism in America. He writes:

> This wasn't about white guilt. (God made me white, and I'm fine with that.) It wasn't about self-loathing, nor was it about political correctness, which has never been important to me. It was simply coming to understand how other people in God's family, precious people, specifically black people, had experienced life very differently than I had. What I learned came from listening to people who loved Jesus as much as I do.[5]

The first step in reconciliation is recognizing that there are people who love Jesus deeply but have a different perspective than we do. This difference of opinion is based on factors such as cultural background, upbringing, life experiences, and even personality. I fully believe divisions over this issue and many others—especially those that divide brothers and sisters in Christ—are the result of an unseen spiritual battle. I'm reminded again of Ephesians 6:12, which says that "our struggle is not against flesh and blood." Satan wages war on the saints to hinder God's work in and through them as much as possible. I think we are wise when we recognize that and actively—even forcefully—seek unity with fellow Christians.

I think focusing on the semantics and the words people are using to communicate keeps us focused on what's happening on this earth when something so much bigger is going on. Like justice, unity is also something God cares about deeply. I have read about the Day of Pentecost in Acts 2 more times than I can count. I have always been fascinated by the account of the wind blowing and the tongues of fire coming down on the Jewish believers. But something else was going on that day. The Bible says there were "God-fearing Jews from every nation under heaven" in that crowd (verse 5). Perhaps because of the events of early 2020, and the conversations (and arguments) that were dominating the societal landscape at the time, that particular detail of the story really stood out to me. I had never paid much attention to the description of the crowd found in verses 9–11: "Parthians, Medes and Elamites; residents of Mesopotamia, Judea and Cappadocia, Pontus and Asia, Phrygia and Pamphylia, Egypt and the parts of Libya near Cyrene; visitors from Rome (both Jews and converts to Judaism); Cretans and Arabs."

The author of Acts, Luke the physician, takes great pains to describe the many nationalities gathered to receive the Holy Spirit. I wondered why God made a point to tell us very specifically what kind of people were there—the diversity represented. This is one of those musings I would love to discuss with Jesus under a tree when I finally make it *home*. For now, from my personal study and prayer, I think God wants us to know that diversity is part of His big plan of reconciliation between God and mankind. It's not about one skin color, country, or ethnic group. It's powerful that God chose to pour out His Spirit at a time and place where all the known nations and languages were present. How beautiful and telling of the heart of the Father.

When I think of how Jesus spent His last moments in prayer, I am struck by further evidence of His desires. We catch a glimpse into His petitions to His Father before taking that torturous walk to the cross. After Jesus prayed for His disciples, He interceded for all of His disciples, both present and future. Yes, Jesus prayed for you and me! Of all the things He could have said to the Father, I think it is important to notice *what* He asked the Father to do in us: "I pray also for those who will believe in me through their message, that all of them may be one, Father, just as you are in me and I am in you. May they also be in us so that the world may believe that you have sent me" (John 17:20–21). Jesus prayed for unity!

One of the shortest psalms in scripture, Psalm 133, begins, "How good and pleasant it is when God's people live together in unity!" and concludes, "For there the LORD bestows his blessing, even life forevermore" (verses 1 and 3). There's something about unity that leads to blessing and to people knowing Jesus. It's no wonder that the principalities of darkness would do all they can to squelch unity among the people of God.

As the apostle Paul established, true unity is seen in diversity—the different sexes, skin tones, languages, cultural histories, and practices. God expresses Himself through diversity. I always marvel at His creativity in things like the animals He created. How boring would a zoo be if there were just dogs in every enclosure? Instead, when I see apes and then zebras and then giraffes (which I am convinced show God's sense of humor), I am moved by our Creator's awesome creativity. Similarly, He has created all different kinds of people. Yes, in different shades and with different languages, but even beyond that: math geniuses, musicians, scientists, creatives, children, those with disabilities, etc.

We can even see this diversity on a friendship level. I love having a plan and a schedule; one of my spiritual gifts is administration. My friend Laura has the gift of hospitality and can make any space or table look beautiful. My friend Tammy has an organization business, and her happiest place on earth is The Container Store. Each of us is wildly different from one another, but we all love Jesus (and each other) and long to use our gifts for Him.

There's something so beautiful about the body of Christ. God created us to need each other. Satan has done a good job convincing the eyes that they are better than the hands, and telling the heads that they don't need the feet. Unity in diversity is such a huge part of what God wants to do in the lives of His children that the enemy wants to demolish it using any means necessary. But we can't fight darkness with more darkness; the only way to defeat darkness is by letting in the light.

DARK SIDE OF SOCIAL MEDIA

In 2020, as issues erupted while we were all physically separated, it often felt like digital communication seemed to pour gasoline on the already burning flame. It didn't feel adequate for discussing such deep heart matters. When he researched his novel, Randy Alcorn met face-to-face with dozens of Black Christians. I'm sure hearing their stories in person—taking in the tones of their voices, seeing their facial expressions or their eyes welling up, perhaps hearing their voices crack with emotion—was much more impactful than exchanging words in a comment section. Unfortunately, with a global pandemic going on, we lacked the luxury of talking in person about what we were feeling, which created tension and misunderstandings on both sides. As I witnessed the online battles, I kept thinking, *My life matters.* And I wondered why it felt so controversial to say so.

As I've spent more time in the world of digital communication, I've observed that a primary way the enemy gets the better of us is through miscommunication. This is apparent in our world, in a time when people seem divided over more issues than ever before. It's also evident in online communication. Whether someone is criticizing my hair (now natural and curly), my weight, my beloved Tennessee Titans, or my beliefs, I am learning to follow a protocol: Get clarification, seek to understand, and offer grace. This doesn't come naturally for me. Quite the opposite, in fact. Sometimes a hurtful comment has caused heat to shoot up my spine like a thermometer. I have spent more time than I care to admit coming up with the perfect response and creating a fictional back-and-forth argument in my mind. But after working myself into a tizzy, the slightest pause would often allow the Holy Spirit to grab my attention and reveal the fact that I had been debating a wall.

When I choose to "tattle" on that person to God instead, my rising anger inevitably subsides. Sometimes I even begrudgingly let it go. Every now and then, I feel led to seek clarification from the person posting. And I am surprised and humbled by how often I have mis-understood what the person was trying to express. I am also caught off guard by how liberating it feels to simply and respectfully agree to disagree in love.

When I encounter negative comments, I have to stand firm in what God says about me. Otherwise, all those other voices—positive and negative—start to define me. At times I've had to take a social media break because I know I'm sensitive and have a difficult time handling what people might say about me. My skin is growing thicker, but I am a work in progress. Lysa TerKeurst has said, "Don't let people's compliments go to your head, and don't let their criticisms go to your heart. The degree to which you do either of these things is the degree to which you'll be ruled by what other people think of you."[6]

When I allow myself to be ruled by others' approval, I lose my effectiveness as an ambassador of Christ. Jesus is my true King, and as a Christian artist I have an opportu-nity to share His truth with others. My mentor Dave says:

"In whose ears are your words big?" We all have people like that in our lives. They could be our children, our coworkers, or people we serve at church. As I engage with my online audience, I realize people are listening. People who are questioning their worth and identity; people who are battling anxiety and depression; people who have been hurt and feel more brave behind the anonymity of a computer screen. Our words are so powerful. We can use them to speak life or death. I choose life.

But in the wake of the many tensions of 2020, feelings I'd experienced throughout my life of not fitting in returned. Here I was, a public figure in Christian contemporary music—a genre dominated by white singers—while also an African American woman. I felt pressure from both sides to say the right things, and yet I felt unable to satisfy either. That's when I realized that though being a Black woman and a CCM singer were both *parts* of my identity, I was not responsible for carrying the banner for either aspect of myself. First and foremost, I am a representative of Christ. As such, I have been entrusted with the ministry of reconciliation. 2 Corinthians 5:20 puts it this way: "We are therefore Christ's ambassadors, as though God were making his appeal through us. We implore you on Christ's behalf: Be reconciled to God."

I love that! The other parts of my identity are important, but my identity as a servant of the Most High God is *most* important. The ministry of reconciliation between God and the people He loves is my true mission, and it's the one that will last into eternity. Sometimes that means speaking up when I see injustice. And an opportunity to do so came along sooner than I expected.

THE LETTER

In June 2020, I listened to an inspiring message my friend Kristi McLelland shared at her church, Church of the City in Franklin. Kristi teaches from a Middle Eastern perspective, and it was her Bible study, *Jesus and Women*, that first opened my eyes to how God feels about justice and righteousness. As Kristi shared about the influence God had given her for such a time as this, she recognized that along with that influence came responsibility. Knowing Kristi, both onstage and off, I was familiar with how she was leveraging her influence for the benefit of God's kingdom.

After hearing that sermon, I thought about the favor God had given me as a Black woman in the CCM community. Radio stations, listened to by predominately white Americans, played my music and gave me a voice through interviews on their stations. I hoped my influence could help make a positive change.

As I prayed about how God wanted me to leverage my unique position, an idea began to form in my mind. Of the top thirty songs on the adult contemporary Christian chart at the time, only two were by people of color. I planned to write a letter to Christian radio personnel, asking them to consider playing more songs by people of color.

Days and then weeks passed as I procrastinated. During my prayer times, I felt that little nudge from the Holy Spirit, but I continued to put it off. I came to understand I was battling fear. I worried that stations would be offended and that my intent would be misunderstood. When I finally brought that concern to God, He graciously gave me the idea for a different approach. Rather than simply sending a written letter, I would read it on camera. I hoped the visual along with my words would present a fuller picture of my heart and motives. To make it more of a conversation, I asked my record label to set up a time for radio stations to dialogue with me afterward.

After writing and tweaking and praying, I was ready. With my Havanese dog, Kiya, sitting on my lap for emotional support (more about her later), I recorded a video of myself reading the letter I had written. "I hope you can see my heart in my eyes," I said as I began the seven-minute recording. Here is part of the letter I read:

Dear radio friends,

May 2020 marked thirteen years that you have played me on your stations. After American Idol, *I remember questioning whether or not I would be accepted in the contemporary Christian music world; after all, most of the artists that I heard on my local CCM stations didn't look or sound much like me. But I will never forget walking through the halls of GMA Week. All of a sudden, I heard my debut single, "Only the World," on full blast. Over a decade later, I tear up every time I hear one of my songs on one of your stations. It's not something I take for granted, and I can't tell you how thankful I am for your support.*

I remember an event that my record label, Sparrow Records, put on during GMA Week that year. One of my most poignant memories of that event was TobyMac standing before you imploring you to play me on your stations. It was honestly hard for me to accept all the kind words he was speaking about me.

But looking back now, I understand that he was championing me because he understood the beauty of diversity. It's almost as if Toby could see the impact this could have in the kingdom. I don't think in that moment I could see the same.

In the years since that event, I have come to see it, I went on to explain. I saw it when at a radio interview, I heard an audio clip of a former Ku Klux Klan member saying she had cut ties with the organization after hearing my music and interviews on Christian radio. God had used my presence there to soften her heart and change some racist views she held about Black people. That interview had left an indelible mark on me.

In the letter I talked about Jesus's prayer for unity among His followers in John 17, and the diversity we see on the Day of Pentecost in Acts 2. I quoted Reverend Martin Luther King Jr. as I addressed how the tragic events of recent months had added "deeper darkness to a night already devoid of stars." Those tragedies, I said, were not new to me or to the Black community. What felt new to me was the response I had personally seen from my white brothers and sisters, both publicly and privately. "Once upon a time, cries for justice came from people who look like I do," I wrote. "But this time feels different.

I've never felt such hope that the walls of racism and division could finally be torn down. I believe God is doing a new thing. I want to implore you to leverage the influence you have in your community. I'm asking you to purposely play more artists of color on your stations."

I provided them with a list of five artists and songs by people of color that I thought would fit the CCM format. I asked them to listen to the songs and pray about their role in pursuing unity through diversity in CCM radio. Then I offered them a day for interviews where we could have an honest conversation about the issues we were facing: July 23, 2020.

When I hit send on that email, I didn't know what to expect. I breathed a sigh of relief when the response was overwhelmingly positive. As planned, I did a full day of radio interviews on Zoom. Then my label asked if I could do another day. "More people want to talk to you," they said. Then a third day was requested. I was so encouraged. When I sent the letter, I had wondered if I were sealing my fate of being ousted from Christian music, but the opposite occurred. Dozens of people thanked me for addressing an important issue that was riddled with relational landmines.

"Mandisa's letter is exactly how I've been feeling for two years," one radio personality wrote. "Super affirming."

Another wrote, "Thanks to Mandisa for speaking out about this. We've had conversations about this at the station and have hope things will change for the better. I appreciate your prayers for wisdom."

A Black female radio employee wrote: "Oh my sweet Jesus! Thank you, Lord. Kingdom minded—yes and yes! In tears here. Breakthrough. An answer to prayer. One step at a time. Walls are crumbling down."

I was moved by how the call for unity in diversity was resonating with fellow believers. It was clear that God was working in this area. I received a message on Twitter from a radio personality whom I had befriended. She thanked me for being brave and wondered if I had the same conversation with record labels asking them to sign more Black artists. I responded that I felt comfortable having that conversation with *my* label but thought we could pray about continuing the dialogue with the others. Shortly after that, another radio friend in St. Louis, Missouri, said that before she received my letter, she had felt a burden to write a letter to record labels with the exact request. Like me, she had dragged her feet out of fear. When she received my letter, she said, she knew God was directing her to follow through on writing her letter—and she did!

That is the beauty of the family of God. As we listen to the Holy Spirit's prompting and step forward in obedience, our actions bring light to the darkness and create a domino effect in others. For years, many people had been praying for someone to start the conversation on diversity in Christian music, and I was one puzzle piece God used to accomplish His purposes. In a place where there had been division—Black gospel, Southern gospel, CCM—God reminded us that it's *all* gospel. It's all about Jesus.

I fully believe God is calling His children to be bridges across divisive issues like racial injustice. When you're a bridge, you have to be willing to be walked on by both sides. When I receive insensitive comments after sharing about my personal experiences feeling marginalized because of my race, that hurts. The time when I was doing a live video on Instagram and someone called me the n-word, it bothered me tremendously. It also bothered me when a Black woman commented under one of my posts that as one of a few Black artists in my industry, I was not saying and doing enough.

I've learned that you can't please everyone. What I *can* do is be a bridge—and I think that's part of what God has called me to be.

Maybe you're thinking, *That's great for Mandisa, but what can I do?* I think asking that question is a great place to start. Regardless of your circle of influence, you can be an advocate for unity in Christ through diversity. Think about how you can leverage the influence you have to benefit the kingdom. Maybe that means inviting your Black coworker to dinner and having a conversation. It could mean befriending someone who doesn't look like you or was raised differently. Perhaps it means speaking up when someone makes an insensitive comment or tells a joke about someone from a different culture while everyone else laughs. Maybe it means starting an awkward conversation or asking hard questions and choosing to really listen and understand someone else's perspective.

I don't think there's one right response. But as followers of Jesus, we need to talk to Jesus about it. He'll make the way. If He's prompting you to do something, do it! Obedience doesn't mean you'll get the response you want or expect. But as you seek after what God values, you grow closer to Him and gain a richer perspective of the diversity represented in God's family.

WAY MAKER

In 2020 I released my version of a song that was making its rounds in Christian music. I first heard "Way Maker" at my church, and the lyrics had a profound effect on me. In my private times of worship, I would often sing it to

God as part of my prayer time. I loved the way the song declared so many facets of God's nature.

Another thing I loved about the song was how I was seeing so many beautiful expressions of it—from Michael W. Smith and Leeland to William McDowell and Darlene Zschech. I heard it in English, Spanish, and even German, with churches around the world proclaiming who God is in their own language. To me, at a time of so much division, it reminded me that it is our Father who brings us all together in His name.

In October 2020, I had the honor of performing at the Dove Awards with Leeland and with Sinach, the Nigerian worship leader who wrote and originally sang "Way Maker." We were also joined by Maverick City Music, an ethnically diverse group of worshippers who had quickly become some of my favorites. I imagine that God's heart leaped as this beautiful variety of Jesus-followers gathered together, lifting up His name. As we sang "Way Maker" together, I was reminded of the One who makes a way in the wilderness.

Even now, God is making a way for His glory to be seen among every ethnic group in the world and through the breathtaking, unexplainable unity of believers. We are Team Jesus—on mission to invite others into a saving relationship with Him. God invites us, regardless of the color of our skin, to be ambassadors and ministers of reconciliation, to be bridges. That's not always a comfortable place, but we can be sure He is with us every step of the way. He's the light in the darkness.

Getting Real

- How can the concept of "coming to the table" and having face-to-face conversations aid our conversations about racial injustice and other divisive issues?
- Read Ephesians 6:12. In what ways do you think the unseen spiritual battle plays into disunity among believers?
- I felt prompted to write a letter to Christian radio, pointing out the lack of diversity and opening up a discussion about racial issues. Talk about a time when you felt prompted to do something difficult or awkward for the benefit of the kingdom.
- Think of a time when you attempted to facilitate reconciliation between two opposing groups. What happened? How did God walk with you through that?
- What is one way you can leverage your influence to facilitate greater unity within the body of Christ?

eleven

YOU KEEP HOPE ALIVE

Days may be darkest
But Your light is greater
You light our way
God, You light our way
When evil is rising
You're rising higher
With power to save
With power to save
You keep hope alive

When our mayor first issued a "safer at home" order on March 23, 2020, I was skeptical. Like many others, I thought this whole coronavirus thing was being blown out of proportion and figured life would be back to normal in a few weeks. The mayor's order was supposed to last two weeks and end on April 6. Of course, we all know what happened.

As more information about the virus came to light and the order was extended, I knew I might be in trouble. Many of my remaining tour dates were postponed and several were cancelled. Sporting events ceased, businesses closed, and kids came home from school. I'm not a fan of the unknown. I may have even been accused of being a "control freak" once or twice in my life. I would defend myself, saying I just like to know what's happening around me. The pandemic, however, was like nothing I had ever experienced before, and it really pushed me to my limit.

As a single woman living alone, I felt particularly vulnerable to depression, loneliness, and other mental health struggles as the pandemic set in. I had two choices: I could go my usual route during stressful circumstances— self-isolating and eating—or I could forge a different path.

You may have heard that the definition of insanity is doing the same thing over and over again and expecting a different result. Proverbs puts it this way: "As a dog returns to its vomit, so fools repeat their folly" (Proverbs 26:11). Don't you just love the Bible? Seriously, that is imagery you can't unsee, and the point is very true. It is human nature to repeat our mistakes—get stuck in a rut or the same old patterns when life gets stressful. Our coping mechanisms are formed during childhood and become more and more set—like cement drying—throughout our lives. Moving past our foolish ways requires a plan and commitment to strike out on a new path. Think about it: Rarely do we just stumble into losing weight, overcoming an addiction, or saving a strained relationship. These feats require intentionality, resolve, and hard work.

As the bad news about the pandemic grew, and as weeks turned into months, I began to notice the warning signs of impending darkness, the same kind I'd experienced after Kisha died. To chip away at the dried cement around my usual coping mechanisms, I intentionally reached out to my friends—many of the same people who had helped me come out of the dark. We needed each other more than ever. I also realized I could provide hope to others who might be struggling.

MUSIC OF HOPE

That year I released three worship singles: "Way Maker," "You Keep Hope Alive," and "It's Not Over." These were my first singles since the 2017 release of my *Out of the Dark* album. Although these songs weren't the CCM R&B-style anthems I was known for, they were hymns of hope to remind us of God's faithfulness during a year marked by disappointments and uncertainties. I had felt a pull toward worship music ever since it had been a lifeline for me in my journey out of the darkness of depression.

The song "You Keep Hope Alive" was especially important to me. I originally met songwriter Jon Reddick through his sister, Janice Gaines, who used to sing background vocals for me. Later, Jon traveled on the road as part of my band playing keys. On the worship staff at Church of the City in Franklin, Tennessee, Jon and I shared in common being one of a few Black people. We had become friends, and his song "You Keep Hope Alive" was one of my favorites. The story of how the song came to be was something I could identify with. He wrote it shortly after the August 12, 2017, terrorist attack in Charlottesville, Virginia. On that day, a twenty-year-old man with neo-Nazi and white supremacist beliefs drove his car into a group of peaceful protestors, killing one and injuring nineteen. "I wanted to have a song to sing in hopeless moments," Jon said in an interview. "After that incident, I had so many questions and emotions; so much sadness and hurt. My son was twelve at the time. And I couldn't figure out why somebody would hate him before they got to know him."

He says that later that week, while in a writing session, a friend sang the line, "You keep hope alive." The statement resonated with Jon, and he wrote the song.

You keep hope alive
You keep hope alive
From the beginning to end
You Word never fails
You keep hope alive
Because You are alive
Jesus, You are alive

He began singing it at his church and was amazed to hear stories of people using it as a prayer for the hard times they were going through. He realized hope is a weapon, and as a Christian you can march against everything that wants to stop you with the weapon of hope in your hand.

When my label approached me about recording a new version of the song, I asked Jon if we could sing it together. It was released in May of that year. With God imprinting the message of unity in the body of Christ on both of our hearts, Jon and I released a few other versions of the song. In the Unity International Version, we asked some friends to join us. Together we proclaimed the power of hope in English, Spanish, Xhosa, Italian, Tagalog, Haitian Creole, and Mandarin. With everything going on in the world, the song's message of hope was poignant. It was a reminder that God was still on His throne and bringing beauty from ashes.

I recorded my vocals for "You Keep Hope Alive" shortly after Easter weekend. I'm sure that's why, as I meditated on the message of hope, a story in scripture came to mind. Every year I heard so much about Good Friday and Easter Sunday, but in that year like no other, I found myself thinking about Saturday. I knew it was Sabbath, and I found myself wondering what the disciples actually felt on that day.

After hundreds of years of the Jewish people crying out to God to save them, the disciples had put their hope in Jesus to be their long-awaited Messiah. His teachings may have been unorthodox, but they had seen Him do things no mere mortal could do. Even as He was taken into captivity, beaten, mocked, and nailed to the cross, I wonder if they still held out hope. Maybe James and John, the "Sons of Thunder," expected Jesus to call down battle-ready angels from heaven in a dramatic show of force. Maybe as John stood near the cross with Mary, he waited for Jesus to say, "Are you ready, My beloved disciple?" and imagined the nails that pinned His rabbi to the cross miraculously dissolving into ash. Whatever those early followers of Jesus thought would happen, their hope must have vanished as they watched our Savior breath His last.

The Bible doesn't say much about what happened right after that. Could they sleep that night? When the sun rose over Golgotha on Saturday morning, did it only bring with it dark memories of what happened the previous day? Were they alone and isolated, or did they gather together and share stories of what they thought was going to happen next? Did they cry or hold in their disappointment? If I had to guess, on a scale of one to ten signifying the disciples' level of hope at that moment, I would speculate it was one or lower.

I started asking myself the same questions. What was I doing with the disappointment of 2020? I had come into the year with a fresh vision of what God would do. My band and I even wore sweatshirts, designed by my friend Katie Haskell, declaring a 20/20 vision. Inscribed with Psalm 20:7, the sweatshirts proclaimed that we trusted in the name of the Lord our God. That truth was much easier to declare in January than by the middle of the year. On that scale of one to ten, where would I have rated *my* hope?

I am so thankful the story didn't end on Saturday. As the disciples gathered together on Sunday, can you imagine how the mood in the room shifted when Jesus suddenly appeared to them? I'm sure their disbelief and then joy could not be contained. How wonderful that like the disciples, we can have hope at any time or in any place simply because Jesus lives. So many times in my life, I've failed to connect with the hope God offers me and focused instead on circumstances that seem hopeless. In Romans 15:13, Paul writes, "May the God of hope fill you with all joy and peace as you trust in him, so that you may overflow with hope by the power of the Holy Spirit."

That verse gives us a few pointers about living in hope. The first is that God is a God of hope. Just knowing Him should give us hope. Second, He delivers hope, joy, and peace as we *trust in Him.* That can be the difficult part. Surrendering our worries and the hard parts of our lives is easier said than done. It's one thing to trust Him on the good days, when things are going our way; it is quite another to trust Him with the scary diagnosis, frightening current events, or the wayward child.

The last part of Romans 15:13 really grabs my attention: "so that you may overflow with hope by the power of the Holy Spirit." This verse is not just talking about a small ration of hope; it's talking about so much hope that it overflows! This kind of hope is only possible through the power of the Holy Spirit. It's the hope God wants us to experience and the devil wants to eradicate. When I let my circumstances dictate my hope, I will never be filled with peace and joy and overflowing with hope.

During my time on the road with Beth Moore, I adopted the "Beth-ism" of turning scripture into prayer. Romans 15:13 is a fantastic verse to do that with: *God of hope—I pray that You would fill me with all joy and peace as I trust in You, so that I may overflow with hope by the power of the Holy Spirit.*

During the pandemic, it became so clear that the world needs hope. Mental health in America seemed to hit rock bottom. One news article reported that 40 percent of Americans were grappling with at least one mental health or drug-related problem, while among young adults that number rose to 75 percent. During that time the Centers for Disease Control and Prevention asked a group of young adults if they had thought about killing themselves in the past thirty days, and one in four said they had. During that time, a very dear friend of mine took his own life. It was hard to not feel hopeless.

Throughout our country and the world, people were grieving the loss of things that made them feel like life was worth living: going out with friends, playing sports, attending concerts, visiting family members, or even just going to school or the office. With these things ripped away, we were all forced to find new ways to cope. As Christians, we had no choice but to take a closer look at where our joy and purpose comes from and how we should react when life doesn't go according to plan.

SPREADING HOPE

As the days grew darker, I was aware of how powerful a flash of light would be. Not only would encouraging others in this unknown time benefit them, but it would also help me. People needed the hope that only comes from Jesus. I decided to use my platform on social media to honestly talk about my own quarantine journey, so that I might encourage others who had similar struggles. The first day of Nashville's stay-at-home order, I jumped on YouTube and streamed my first *Mornings with Mandisa*. Every Monday morning for many consecutive weeks, I would hop on YouTube and share the things God was teaching me. I sang, I danced, I taught, and I prayed. My favorite part of each video was watching and responding to the comments of those who joined me live. At a time when so many of us felt disconnected, that time connecting with others through my computer screen became the highlight of my week.

Eventually those videos morphed into *Mornings with Mandisa & Friends*, where some friends joined me and we discussed topics like health and weight loss, overcoming offense, quarantine anxiety, and praising God through sorrow. I didn't hide the pain I was feeling over things going on in the world, or the sense of loss and grief accompanying my present circumstances. I wanted those videos to feel like I was inviting people to the table. The table is a place where we can lament, a place we can process pain, a place where we can confess our sins and receive healing, a place where we can be refreshed, and a place where we can meet God and receive His comfort through our brothers and sisters in Christ. Even though I didn't have it all figured out, I wanted to share what God was teaching me. It was an "in-process" kind of knowledge.

I also led an online study of *Experiencing God*, the study I had done at Fisk that had led to my job at Lifeway. I asked my friends Chandra (who had first introduced me to the study), Christian, and Mariah to help me lead. Four hundred people from around the world logged on as we led the thirteen-week study. I loved having an opportunity to teach and encourage others through a study that had been so instrumental in my own faith journey. It was one of those full-circle experiences that only comes around a few times in your life.

I also hosted a talk show on YouTube called *What If We Were Real?* For season one, we did a twelve-episode series about relationships. I invited guests, some single and some married, to discuss topics such as communication, sex/purity, gender roles, and interracial dating. I loved "getting my Oprah on" and moderating these kinds of conversations. I'm nosy, and anytime someone is telling me a story, I always have a gazillion questions. This was a way to put that trait to good use!

While we're on the topic of relationships, can we talk about singleness for a minute? I am a single woman, but I love talking about relationships. I think it's incredible that God created marriage and the opportunity for two to become one and serve Him together. In the song "Praying for You" (on my *Overcomer* album), I express some of my thoughts about the man I believe God will bring to me one day:

> For now, I'm waiting, anticipating
> Baby, I know that you'll be
> The one that's strong when I am weak
> I'll love you through the good and the bad
> For rich or for poor
> May not have much but this I'm sure
> Until my dream comes true
> I'll be praying for you
> Praying for you

That is not just a lyric. I actually do pray for my future husband. When the loneliness sets in, I often combat it by talking to God about this man I haven't met yet. (At least, I don't *think* we've met. Who knows? Maybe he's reading this book!) As I mentioned, I love turning scripture into prayers. My favorite passage to cover my husband with is Psalm 112. I pray that he would fear the Lord and find delight in His commands. I pray that he would be gracious, compassionate, and righteous. I pray that he would be generous and conduct his affairs with justice. I pray that he would have a servant's heart and be humble. And if he happens to be a big, Black man, with a bald head and a goatee, that would be a bonus! Regardless of how God answers, I know He hears my prayers and sees my needs.

In his sermon series *The New Rules for Love, Sex, and Dating*, Andy Stanley tells singles that instead of looking for Mr. or Mrs. Right, they should focus on becoming Mr. or Mrs. Right. One way to do this, he says, is by praying through 1 Corinthians 13 for yourself: "Love is patient, love is kind. It does not envy, it does not boast, it is not proud" (verse 4). As I have prayed for God to develop these qualities in my life, I have learned that if you pray for patience, you had better be prepared to be put in situations that test your patience. But growing in these areas now will only serve my future relationship better down the road. As singles develop these loving characteristics in their lives, they are setting themselves up for greater success in relationships, including marriage. I can use 1 Corinthians 13 as a template for becoming a loving person—and someday, Lord willing, a loving spouse.

Like many single women my age, I assumed I'd be married by now. Proverbs 13:12 says, "Hope deferred makes the heart sick, but a longing fulfilled is a tree of life." So many times I have felt the heartsickness this passage describes. But singleness has been one more thing that drives me deeper into my relationship with God. I know He loves me and has wonderful plans for my life. Just like other areas of my life, I know God can provide a spouse if that's His will for me. I do, however, like the idea of Jesus setting me aside just for Himself in the meantime.

Around half of the adult population in the US is married. That means I'm not the only single out there. I'm sure many of you reading this book are representin' for the single ladies and fellas. I don't know your story, but maybe you've experienced some heartsickness in your love life too. I want to encourage you that God is bigger than any unfulfilled longing. He can soothe your loneliness and be your portion. And to all the single ladies, I love the words of Isaiah 54:5: "For your Maker is your husband—the LORD Almighty is his name—the Holy One of Israel is your Redeemer; he is called the God of all the earth." What an incredible privilege to be invited into an intimate relationship with the One who created me and knows me best.

One of the pandemic blessings I found was "going on a date with Jesus." I know that sounds kind of corny, but hear me out. The more I meditated on Isaiah 54 and 1 Corinthians 7, the more I found that God satisfied the deep longing in my heart to be pursued. When I sensed a "woe is single me" pity party coming along, I squashed it by taking a long walk, talking honestly with God about my hurt, and singing to Him. I discovered a little pond by my place, and I could sit there for hours watching the ducks. I'd let the sun beam down on my face and have a heart-to-heart conversation with the Lover of my soul. I never really made time to do that when my schedule was filled with recording, touring, and interviewing. This new rhythm I discovered while the world was essentially shut down is something I hope to take with me for the rest of my life, even when I am married.

PRAISE PUPPY

Growing up, I never had a pet. I didn't give it much thought. My mom was never really a fan of animals, and I suppose I adopted her mindset. When the subject arose, she would turn up her nose as if actually smelling a wet dog odor. I did have a couple of unfortunate experiences with cats, including a cat allergy, that removed all desire for a feline friend. And the little black dog that chased me when I was eight and caused me to flip my bike was traumatic enough for me to also write off "man's best friend." I would stick with two-legged, English-speaking pals, thank you very much. That is, until I met Kiya.

February 18, 2020, is a day I'll never forget. It was my friend Sydni's birthday, and her mom, Jillian, also my friend, lived nearby. I drove to Jillian's house to drop off a gift for Sydni, knowing she would be there celebrating that night. Jillian invited me in to see a litter of Havanese puppies that had been born ten days earlier. With mom Bella protectively looking on, Jillian pointed out each of the five puppies by name. In the litter of mostly light-colored pups, I could almost hear the opening strains to "Circle of Life" when Jillian lifted up the one black puppy. I remember it now in slow motion. As Jillian raised her up, the adorable Kiya raised her paws in the air as if she were praising! I couldn't believe it. That magical moment, meeting my little "praise puppy," convinced me that Kiya had to be part of my life.

Although she had already been named, I was free to give Kiya a different name, but when I looked up the meaning of *Kiya*, I found phrases like "jovial lady," "friend," "happy," and "gift given by God." I couldn't think of a better name! On April 16, after I had been home alone for almost a month, Kiya came home with me and changed my life.

My life wasn't the only thing that changed; so did Kiya. Within months, Kiya's soft coat transformed from black to completely white! Jillian likes to say she tricked me. Despite her color change, and with plenty of time to bond and train, my pandemic puppy soon became my biggest blessing. I discovered her just as the loneliness of quarantine life really began to set in.

And God knew I needed her.

God continues to use Kiya to teach me things about His character. The first time I had to give her a bath, she did not enjoy the experience. She was trembling, crying, and looking at me with those sad puppy-dog eyes. I wrapped her in a towel and put her in her crate to try to calm her down. I was sure she would be upset with me, but when I opened the crate a short time later, she ran to me and wanted to be as close to me as possible. I heard God saying, *This is how I want you to respond to Me, Mandisa. Even when you're upset with Me.* I was struck by the truth that when we're fearful and confused by what's happening, God wants our default to be running straight to Him to hide in the shadow of His wings.

When Kiya was little, I always carried her up the stairs. One day, after arriving home from a walk, I ran up the stairs to see if Kiya would follow. Her frightened whines were enough to send this protective dog-mom back down the stairs, but I knew she could do it. I placed her furry little paws on the first stair and cheered her on to victory. She was hesitant at first, but with a resolve to accomplish something she had never done before, her confidence grew with each step. Now she bounds up the stairs, her fear a distant memory. It reminded me that sometimes when we feel like we can't do something, or we're afraid to, God will give us a little assist. Then He asks us to take the next step, always there to catch us if we falter.

Kiya has brought me joy and given me greater purpose in my life. I've never been a morning person, but now I have to get up each day and take Kiya for a walk. I must care for her needs and provide for her. I love just watching her and seeing all the cute things she does. Her post-bath "zoomies"—where she zooms from corner to corner of my house in three seconds flat—always elicit a heart-laugh. My joy over Kiya is just a small reflection of how my heavenly Father feels about me. And He has been good to remind me of that, through the blessing of a sweet, furry friend.

As I think back on the past few years and the many surprises I've faced, both good and bad, I am deeply aware of God's provision. In many ways, I have left behind some old ways of doing things and struck out on a new path. I've made some mistakes, but God has been faithful to be near in every challenge I've encountered. From beginning to end, He never fails. He keeps hope alive.

Getting Real

- Think of a time when it felt like your world turned upside down. What did you learn through that experience?
- Read Romans 13:15. What are some ways you can connect with the hope God offers?
- "Hope deferred makes the heart sick, but a longing fulfilled is a tree of life" (Proverbs 13:12). Talk about a time when you were heartsick or a time when God fulfilled a longing.
- God offers us perfect love and intimacy regardless of our "relationship status." What are some ways you have found to connect with the Lord and allow Him to show you His love?
- Getting my dog, Kiya, became an unexpected joy during a difficult year. Think of a time when God sent you encouragement at just the right time. What happened?

·twelve·

BREAKTHROUGH

This is where my heart will beat again
This is where I get set free
This is where Your love is calling me
I'm ready, yeah, I'm ready

To cross over the line
Leave it all behind
Nothing's gonna keep me here
Oh, until I see a change
I'm lifting up Your name
There's freedom in the atmosphere

On a typical day, I've noticed the moment I set my computer to the side and turn off my instrumental music, my dog's ears perk up. Kiya eyes me eagerly as I head to my room to grab my socks and sneakers. As soon as I begin to slide them on, she spins around with excitement. Her percussive yelps intermingle with her panting breaths to show her elation at what she knows is about to happen: her afternoon walk.

I'm always amazed by Kiya's endless enthusiasm for something we do pretty much every day. It was on one such walk that the following thought occurred to me: What are some things in my life that I take for granted— unlike my perky puppy who celebrates a simple stroll through our neighborhood?

As we walked along that day, a gentle breeze kissed my face and sunshine filtered through the trees. Kiya pulled on the leash, investigating every stick and unusual smell. With each step I counted my blessings. *Breath in my lungs. Food in my refrigerator. A bed to sleep in. Clothes to wear.* My thoughts turned to my faithful friends, who had fought for me when I was in the dark. God had used their unwavering care, support, and prayers to give me hope and help me see a way into the light. I thought about my faithful Savior, Jesus, who had been a companion and Way Maker every step of the journey. All at once I was overwhelmed with gratefulness. I felt glad to be alive.

My thoughts wandered to my friend Kisha, the source of so much joy and sadness in my life. I imagined she, too, felt glad to be alive—but in a different way, an eternal way. I will never stop wishing she were still here, or wondering why God chose to take her home so early. And yet, my perspective is different today than the day she died. At one time I didn't see Kisha as an overcomer because she lost her earthly battle with cancer.

A few years after Kisha died, I remember reading Revelation 12, which talks about the end of the earth and Satan's final defeat. Verse 11 caught my attention: "And they overcame [Satan] because of the blood of the Lamb and because of the word of their testimony" (NASB). I had read that verse many times but had never realized that the thought is not finished there. The scripture continues: "and they did not love their life even when faced with death." I felt my spiritual eyes being opened. My view of overcoming had been limited to the temporary world in which I was living. But when I use the measuring stick of eternity, Kisha *did* overcome. She knew where she was going. She overcame through the blood of the Lamb, her Lord and Savior, Jesus Christ. She overcame by her testimony, which continues on long after her final breath. I *know* Kisha is living her best life with Jesus right now. She is an overcomer in the truest sense of the word.

God is teaching me how to be an overcomer too—not just getting through a hard time in my life, but experiencing victory daily through His strength and love. I'm learning I don't have to have it all together, or be the best version of myself, to be an overcomer. I can make mistakes, fall back into old sinful patterns, and still walk in victory. Why? Because overcoming isn't dependent on me. It's dependent on my powerful Savior, whose blood has covered all past, present, and future sin. Thank You, Jesus!

In 2020 I released three worship songs. I consider them worship songs, not because of their slower tempo but because they are vertical in nature. I am singing to God when I say, "*You'll* finish what *You* started." My first release of 2021, the song "Breakthrough," continued the vertical worship but also had a funky get-up-and-dance beat. More than just a feel-good anthem, the song was a celebration of the breakthroughs I've experienced through Jesus. It was also a declaration of hope for breakthroughs to come. I'm ready for God to do a new thing in my life, to fill me up with His joy, strength, and purpose. Some of the lyrics give voice to this desire:

> This is where Your Word takes hold of me
> And this is where my fear lets go
> Your Spirit is alive inside of me
> I'm ready, yes, I'm ready

"Breakthrough" was my proclamation that I want to be alert to what God is doing in my life and where He might be planning to break through. In business there's a term: *up and to the right*. It refers to the company's growth curve. A business's profitability or stock may go up and down, but that's okay if its overall trajectory is up and to the right. I want my life in Christ to be like that. How I'm doing on any given day may go up and down, but His mercies are new every morning. I can confess my sin and walk in victory starting that very moment. By His grace I hope that when I look back on my life at the end, my growth trajectory has been up and to the right. I certainly don't have this relationship with Jesus all figured out. But during the years I've been walking with Jesus, I've discovered some practices that help me move in the right direction.

Feeding on scripture. The Bible is a believer's most powerful tool. It's a weapon for the spiritual battle surrounding us. Ephesians 6:17 calls it the "sword of the Spirit." A soldier would never run into battle without a weapon. The Bible isn't just a book with good sayings and interesting stories; it is a key to experiencing freedom and victory in Christ. When I don't abide in God's Word, I notice a difference in my life. I become duller spiritually and less aware of what God is doing and what He wants from me. I'm more susceptible to the enemy's attacks.

In Psalm 119, David writes about how he loves God's Word, the law. He lists scripture's many benefits in our lives: It keeps us from sin (verse 11), it preserves our lives (verse 25), it strengthens us when we are weary with sorrow (verse 28), it gives us hope (verse 49), it lights our way (verse 105), and it "gives understanding to the simple" (verse 130). The Bible does all of those things and so much more!

When I've had a difficult day, opening up my Bible isn't always appealing. It's easier to sit on the couch and click on my favorite TV show. But think about this: God's Word is so powerful the enemy wants to keep us away from it! That's because God's truth diffuses worries, brings godly perspective, encourages and comforts, and compels us to love and serve others. The same goes for memorized scripture. Years ago, I learned from Beth Moore the power of memorizing scripture. Having God's Word hidden in our hearts is an offensive weapon. If Jesus used it to fight off Satan when He was being tempted in the wilderness, so should I! Even in the moments I was trying to push God out, the Holy Spirit used the verses I had memorized to get my attention. In my darkest moments, God's truth would be coming into my mind in the form of His words straight from the Bible. That's why I've led several scripture memorization challenges through the years. If you are struggling in your walk with God or not feeling close to Him, I encourage you to memorize and meditate on His words.

Running in a pack. Our society seems set up for individualism (even more so in the midst of a pandemic). Something I hear a lot from other Christians is, "I have Jesus, and He's all I need." That's dangerous thinking. Even the Godhead is composed of Father, Son, and Holy Spirit. God created us for interdependence. We need each other. We are the body of Christ (1 Corinthians 12), and a body needs all of its parts. Since I'm an ambivert (both introvert and extrovert), there are times when I long to be with people, but my pull for alone time is also very strong. I know that staying home and binge-watching TV is always going to be a temptation for me. But when I give in to it, I often end up feeling isolated, discouraged, and empty. It's an area where Satan can get a foothold in my life—a spot where he can aim that fiery dart and cause injury. Because of this, I recognize that community won't just happen naturally for me; it's something I have to pursue. Last year, I decided to move from my house in Antioch and across town to Franklin. I did this because my friends live on this side of town, and I wanted to cultivate those relationships.

Maybe some of you are thinking, *How do you get friends like that? Friends who stalk you at the movie theater to sticky-note your car? Friends who keep calling until you pick up? Friends who don't take "fine" for an answer and dig deeper to find out how you really are?* I think God loves it when we come to Him with our emotional and relational needs, not just our physical ones. Many people, myself included, pray for God to provide them with a spouse, but what about praying for Him to provide friends who can encourage us in our lives right now? That's a prayer I believe He loves to answer.

Sometimes forming those meaningful connections with others will take you out of your comfort zone. When Kiya and I meet another dog on our walks, a few polite sniffs eventually lead to an awkward sniff of the rear end. I don't know why dogs introduce themselves to one another that way, but if an awkward moment like that can lead to a lifelong friendship, maybe it's worth it. Don't get me wrong—I am not recommending that you make friends the way my dog does. What I am saying is that God may prompt you to make the first move, which can feel un-comfortable. Asking someone to have coffee or go out for dinner can feel risky, but it can end up being rewarding.

During my life I've been drawn into friendships with all types of people—some very different from me. My tribe has included men, women, single people, married people with kids, millennials, more "seasoned" folks, and every age in between. God has blessed me with a diverse group of people in my life—mentors from my church, singers I've been on tour with, people I went to school with, fellow artists and influencers, stay-at-home moms—and they've come with a variety of skin tones. You learn so much and become a richer person by surrounding yourself with people who are different from you. As I've walked through hard things in my life, I've sometimes been surprised by the people God has used to comfort and help me. At times I get to be there for them too. That's what it's all about.

Showing my scars. I remember hearing something *E! News* co-anchor Giuliana Rancic said after going through a public battle with breast cancer. As she was getting dressed to host the red-carpet event for a fancy awards show, her makeup artist asked if she wanted her to cover the scar from her mastectomy. I was moved when she declined, referring to her scars as her "battle wounds." So many times we want to keep hidden the parts of ourselves that show what we have overcome—or more specifically how God has overcome in our lives. I expressed this idea in my song "What Scars Are For":

These scars aren't pretty
But they're a part of me
And will not ever fade away
These marks tell a story
Of me down in the valley
And how You reached in with Your grace
And healed me

They remind me of Your faithfulness
And all You brought me through
They teach me that my brokenness
Is something You can use
They show me where I've been
And that I'm not there anymore
That's what scars, that's what scars are for

As I've been sharing my story in this book, I've realized that it would be a lot more comfortable to keep some of the uglier parts of the story hidden—not airing out things I regret or for which I feel ashamed. I have toyed with the idea of omitting some parts, or rewriting them, but those are my battle wounds and they're not just for me. They're meant to bring glory to God and benefit others. I am glad that the Bible includes David's indiscretion with Bathsheba, Peter's denial of Christ, Thomas's doubts, and Paul's thorn in the flesh. I am thankful Paul speaks about how he pleaded with the Lord to remove that thorn, to no avail. In the times where I, too, have begged God for something only to receive no for an answer, I find comfort in Paul's words in 2 Corinthians 12:9: "But he said to me, 'My grace is sufficient for you, for my power is made perfect in weakness.' Therefore I will boast all the more gladly about my weaknesses, so that Christ's power may rest on me." We serve a God who uses our thorns, frustrations, and even our scars. Don't you love telling a good scar story? You know, the time you wiped out on your bike as a kid and got that permanent scar on your left knee? I think God wants us to tell each other our scar stories so we know we're not the only ones who have them, and we can see how God can turn our weaknesses into strength.

Praising through pain. Two weeks before I was eliminated on *American Idol,* I sang the Mary Mary song "Shackles." I had sung the song onstage many times before, but this time I was proclaiming it before an audience with a variety of beliefs. I love that the song is honest about how difficult our circumstances can be, and yet it proclaims that *nothing* is too hard for God. That night, with thirty million people watching, I belted out words of gratitude for God's faithfulness and the freedom I have found in Christ.

That was a mountaintop experience. I had no idea that one performance later, I would be eliminated from the show and ridiculed for my words and my beliefs. I would go from feeling valuable and admired to worthless and condemned. I knew I wasn't the first Christian to feel this way. No, this kind of experience goes *way* back. In John 15:18–19, Jesus told His disciples: "If the world hates you, keep in mind that it hated me first. If you belonged to the world, it would love you as its own. As it is, you do not belong to the world, but I have chosen you out of the world. That is why the world hates you."

Anytime I hit a valley in my life, I have a choice. I can pull away from God or I can choose to praise Him. Praise is powerful because it reminds me of who is really in charge—the Lord Most High, who is both just and good. At concerts I've told people: "Don't wait until the battle is over. Shout right now! Praise Him right now!" Even in pain and loss, we can join with Job, who said, "The Lord gave and the Lord has taken away; may the name of the Lord be praised" (Job 1:21).

That can be hard to do, but praise is powerful. When my focus is downward—my eyes pointed toward my feet and the place I currently stand—choosing to "go vertical" and focus above, where Jesus sits at the right hand of the Father, lifts my eyes upward. Worshipping God changes our perspective on our circumstances. It reminds us:

There is no one like our God. (Psalm 113:5)

Nothing is impossible with God. (Mark 10:27)

God's love and faithfulness are steadfast. (Psalm 115:1)

We dwell "in the shelter of the Most High." (Psalm 91:1)

I can praise Him even in the conflict because He fights my battles and the victory has already been secured. Hallelujah! No matter how much I'm struggling, praise turns my eyes away from my situation toward God's unlimited resources. Worshipping the Almighty God gives me strength to stay on the path and hope that everything in my life—including pain and loss—has purpose.

UNFINISHED

To be completely honest, I struggled even while writing this book. Seeing how God has faithfully led me from the day I was born up until now has been encouraging, but revisiting my darkest moments was really heavy. So many of those things still hurt deeply. I have been tempted to walk away from this—showing my scars and telling my scar story.

I have even wondered if I'm qualified for others to learn from and follow. I'm not some Christian "success story." (But when you look at scripture, neither were Abraham, Moses, or David, so I guess I'm in good company!)

Here's why I've persevered: *This is God's story.* It's the story of how God broke into my life when I was sixteen years old and changed everything. It's the story of how He lovingly pursued me at times when I was walking away from Him. It's the story of how He gently guided me every step of the way and gave me opportunities I never could have imagined. It's the story of how He used people to come around me and be instruments of His love and grace, declaring truth over me and not allowing me to stay in the pit.

It's not a story about Mandisa, really. It's a story about a big God who has changed one woman's life in unbelievable ways. He's taken my heart of stone and replaced it with a heart of flesh (Ezekiel 36:26). He's made me a worshipper.

Paul perfectly captures this journey in 2 Corinthians 3:18 when he says, "And we all, who with unveiled faces contemplate the Lord's glory, are being transformed into his image with ever-increasing glory, which comes from the Lord, who is the Spirit." When I was at my lowest point, He knew everything that was ahead. When the enemy sought to take me out, God redeemed my life from the pit and crowned me with love and compassion (Psalm 103:4).

That's my story, and it can be your story too. My song "Unfinished" embodies my current feelings:

> He started something good
> And I'm gonna believe it
> He started something good
> And He's gonna complete it
> So I'll celebrate the truth
> His work in me ain't through
> I'm just unfinished

Unfinished but loving my Lord, my Way Maker, who brought me out of the dark and into His glorious light.

Getting Real

- Describe a time when you felt grateful to be alive. What factors turned your heart and mind toward gratitude?
- According to the Bible, what does it mean to be an overcomer? What insight does Revelation 12:11 give us into the source of our victory as believers?

- Looking back on your journey of knowing God, has your growth been "up and to the right"? If not, what is getting in your way? What are some changes you could make to get on a steady growth curve?
- Do you have a "scar story"—a time when God brought you through something hard or redeemed bad choices in your life? What happened? Is there someone who needs to hear your scar story?
- The Christian life is a process of being transformed into the image of Jesus by small increments. How does this understanding of faith encourage you or change your perspective?

ACKNOWLEDGMENTS

When I experienced my "deep dark" after Kisha passed away, I never imagined God would redeem that valley and give me the opportunity to tell my story to encourage others. He is a master at making beauty from ashes. I'm so incredibly grateful for the team of people the Lord surrounded me with, who offered love, encouragement, talent, and know-how to guide me through the process of creating this book.

Thank you to my family and friends for the unconditional love and support. Shout out to Nicole Staples, Tammy Jensen, and Carine Abraham for coming over while I worked on this just so I wouldn't be alone.

Thanks to my friend Natalie Grant for writing such a gracious and beautiful foreword that truly captures my hopes for this book.

Thank you to my manager, Dan Pitts, and True Artist Management for your encouragement and for translating my deafening silences to those waiting to hear my voice.

Thank you, Suzanne Gosselin, for helping me craft my story. You helped me testify about my life in a way that points people to Jesus and His faithfulness. This process was more difficult than I imagined, and your patience, understanding, and grace was more appreciated than I can express. Thanks for including Kiya the Havi in the writing process. She sends you her love!

Thank you to EMF Director of Publishing Dave Schroeder and CEO Bill Reeves for believing in me and for giving me the opportunity to tell my story. Your kindness, patience, and enthusiasm have been a blessing and an encouragement.

Thank you to Brian Mitchell, President of WTA, for championing the project and making it possible.

Thank you to Matt West, CEO of Dexterity Publishing, and the whole Dexterity team: Lauren Langston Stewart and Jocelyn Bailey for your oversight and expertise, and for all of the hard work you've put into this project.

Thank you to my "fandisas." When I feel insecure about revealing the dark places, your constant messages of hope and encouragement shine brightly. There is hope, my friends.

Finally, to my God, who specializes in making beauty from ashes—I am grateful and hopeful that You will do the same with this offering I place at Your feet.

SONGWRITING CREDITS

"THE ONE HE SPEAKS THROUGH"

Written by Colby Wedgworth, Ben Glover, and Mandisa

© 2017 Colby Wedgeworth Music (ASCAP) / Fair Trade Music Publishing (ASCAP) / (admin at EssentialMusicPublishing.com)

Meaux Hits (ASCAP) Heavenly Melodisa Music (ASCAP) Ariose Music (ASCAP) (adm. at CapitolCMGPublishing.com)

"UNFINISHED"

Written by Wedgeworth and Ben Glover

© 2017 Colby Wedgeworth Music (ASCAP) / Fair Trade Music Publishing (ASCAP) / (admin at EssentialMusicPublishing.com)

Ariose Music (ASCAP) (adm. at CapitolCMGPublishing.com)

"BLEED THE SAME"

Written by Chris Stevens, Bryan Fowler, Toby McKeehan, and Mandisa

© 2017 Moody Producer Music (BMI) Musical Moodswing (SESAC) Achtober Songs (BMI) Meaux Hits (ASCAP) Meaux Mercy (BMI) Heavenly Melodisa Music (ASCAP) Capitol CMG Amplifier (SESAC) (adm. at CapitolCMGPublishing.com)

"MY FIRST LOVE"

Written by Jeremy Camp, Seth Mosley, and Mandisa

© 2017 Only In You Publishing (SESAC) CentricSongs (SESAC) These Tunes Go To 11 (SESAC) Meaux Hits (ASCAP) Heavenly Melodisa Music (ASCAP) (adm. at CapitolCMGPublishing.com)

"BREAKTHROUGH"

Written by Ian Keaggy, Casey Brown, Hope Darst, and Charles Starling

© 2021 Isk Music (ASCAP) / I Used to be in a Metal Band (SESAC) Eight26Publishing (ASCAP) TBCO Music (ASCAP) TBCO Publishing (BMI) Starling and Starling Publishing (APRA) TBCO Songs (SESAC) (adm. at CapitolCMGPublishing.com)

"GOD SPEAKING"

Written by Ronnie Freeman

© 2007 New Spring Publishing Inc. (ASCAP) Lehajoes Music (ASCAP) (adm. at CapitolCMGPublishing.com)

"HE IS WITH YOU"

Written by Cindy Morgan and Ronnie Freeman

© 2009 New Spring Publishing Inc. (ASCAP) Lehajoes Music (ASCAP) Solivia Music Publishing (ASCAP) (adm. at CapitolCMGPublishing.com)

"WHAT SCARS ARE FOR"

Written by Sam Mizell, Jeff Pardo, and Mandisa

© 2013 Centricity Songs (BMI) Meaux Hits (ASCAP) Meaux Jeaux Music (SESAC) Heavenly Melodisa Music (ASCAP) (adm. at CapitolCMGPublishing.com)

W.C.M. MUSIC CORP. All rights on behalf of Curb Dayspring Music administered by Warner-Tamerlane Publishing Corp.

Rizzle Music (ASCAP) Universal Music - Brentwood Benson Publ. (ASCAP) (adm. at CapitolCMGPublishing.com)

"ONLY THE WORLD"

Written by Matthew West, Sam Mizell, and Clint Lagerberg

© 2006 Simple Tense Songs (ASCAP) / Wyzell Music (ASCAP) (both admin. by BMG Rights Mgmt. c/o Music Services, Inc.)

Curb Word Music (ASCAP). All rights on behalf of Curb Word Music administered by WC Music Corp.

"I'M STILL HERE"

Written by Matthew West, AJ Pruis, and Mandisa

© 2017 Meaux Hits (ASCAP) Heavenly Melodisa Music (ASCAP) (adm. at CapitolCMGPublishing.com) permission.

"GOOD NEWS"

Written by Matthew West, AJ Pruis, and Mandisa

© 2017 Meaux Hits (ASCAP) Heavenly Melodisa Music (ASCAP) (adm. at CapitolCMGPublishing.com)

"GOOD MORNING"

Written by Cary Barlowe, Toby McKeehan, Mandisa, Chris Rice, and Jamie Moore

© 2011 Achtober Songs (BMI) Meaux Hits (ASCAP) Jamnu Publishing (ASCAP) Heavenly Melodisa Music (ASCAP) Songs Of Emack (ASCAP) Songs Of Essbearre (SESAC) Songs Of Third Base (SESAC) Universal Music - Brentwood Benson Publ. (ASCAP)

SONGWRITING CREDITS

Universal Music - Brentwood Benson Tunes (SESAC) (adm. at
CapitolCMGPublishing.com)

"OVERCOMER"

Written by Christopher Stevens, Ben Glover, and David Garcia

© 2013 Meaux Mercy (BMI) Moody Producer Music (BMI) Ariose
Music (ASCAP) Universal Music - Brentwood Benson Publ. (ASCAP)
(adm. at CapitolCMGPublishing.com)

"DEAR JOHN"

Written by Mandisa, Sam Tinnesz, and Tiffany Arbuckle-Lee

© 2013 Meaux Hits (ASCAP) Heavenly Melodisa Music (ASCAP)
(adm. at CapitolCMGPublishing.com)

"YOU KEEP HOPE ALIVE"

Written by Paul Baloche, Jess Cates, Jon Reddick, and Anthony Skinner

NOTES

1. Mandisa, *Idoleyes: My New Perspective on Faith, Fat & Fame* (Carol Stream, IL: Tyndale House, 2007), 196–97.
2. "Unmarried and Single Americans Week: September 19-25, 2021," United States Census Bureau, September 20, 2021, https://www.census.gov/newsroom/stories/unmarried-single-americans-week.html.
3. C.S. Lewis, *The Problem of Pain* (New York: HarperOne, 1940), 91.
4. Tim Challies, "I Fear God, and I'm Afraid of God," *Challies* (blog), December 4, 2020, *https*://www.challies.com/articles/i-fear-god-and-i-am-afraid-of-god/.
5. Randy Alcorn, "Black Lives Do Matter, But the BLM Organization Opposes Christian Values: So What Should We Do?" *Eternal Perspective Ministries* (blog), July 20, 2020, https://www.epm.org/blog/2020/Jul/20/black-lives-do-matter.
6. Lysa TerKeurst, *Made to Crave Devotional: 60 Days to Craving God, Not Food* (Grand Rapids, MI: Zondervan, 2011), 53.

ABOUT THE AUTHORS

Contemporary Christian and gospel vocalist, *American Idol* season-five alumna, and author of *Idoleyes: My New Perspective on Faith, Fat & Fame*, Mandisa is a Grammy Award–winning and Dove-nominated artist who got her start singing backup for Trisha Yearwood and Shania Twain.

Her debut album, *True Beauty*, featuring collaborations with the Fisk Jubilee Singers and TobyMac, topped Billboard's Top Christian Albums chart. Her 2013 *Overcomer* won a Grammy for Best Contemporary Christian Music Album.

Mandisa's passions for faith, health and wellness, and mental health are common themes in her writing, both musical and literary. Her fifth full-length album, *Out of the Dark,* was inspired by the death of a close friend and the deep depression that followed.

Mandisa studied vocal jazz at American River College before earning a bachelor's degree in music with a concentration in vocal performance from Fisk University. She now lives in Franklin, Tennessee. *Out of the Dark: My Journey Through the Shadows to Embrace God's Joy* is her second book.

Suzanne Gosselin is a freelance writer and editor. Formerly an editor for *Clubhouse* and *Clubhouse Jr.* magazines, she has written books and devotionals for Zondervan, David C. Cook, Tyndale, and Harvest House. She graduated from Multnomah University with a degree in journalism and biblical theology and has written hundreds of popular articles and blog posts for a variety of periodicals. She lives in California with her husband, Kevin, a family pastor, and four young children. Suzanne enjoys sharing a good cup of coffee and conversation with a friend, serving with her husband in student ministry, and soaking up the beauty of God's creation on the California coast.